Questioning, Instructional Strategies, and Classroom Management

Other Titles by Marie Menna Pagliaro

A Blueprint for Preparing Teachers: Producing the Best Educators for Our Children (2016)

Academic Success: Applying Learning Theory in the Classroom (2013)

Mastery Teaching Skills: A Resource for Implementing the Common Core State Standards (2012)

Research-Based Unit and Lesson Planning: Maximizing Student Achievement (2012)

Differentiating Instruction: Matching Strategies with Objectives (2011)

Educator or Bully: Managing the 21st Century Classroom (2011)

Exemplary Classroom Questioning: Practices to Promote Thinking and Learning (2011)

Questioning, Instructional Strategies, and Classroom Management

A Compendium of Criteria for Best Teaching Practices

Marie Menna Pagliaro

ROWMAN & LITTLEFIELD
Lanham · Boulder · New York · London

Published by Rowman & Littlefield
A wholly owned subsidiary of The Rowman & Littlefield Publishing Group, Inc.
4501 Forbes Boulevard, Suite 200, Lanham, Maryland 20706
www.rowman.com

Unit A, Whitacre Mews, 26–34 Stannary Street, London SE11 4AB

British Library Cataloguing in Publication Information Available

Library of Congress Cataloging-in-Publication Data

ISBN 978-1-4758-3861-9 (cloth : alk. paper)
ISBN 978-1-4758-3862-6 (paperback : alk. paper)
ISBN 978-1-4758-3863-3 (electronic)

♾™ The paper used in this publication meets the minimum requirements of American National Standard for Information Sciences—Permanence of Paper for Printed Library Materials, ANSI/NISO Z39.48–1992.

Printed in the United States of America

Contents

Preface

It has often been said that knowledge is power. But knowledge is useless power unless it can be translated into performance. When teachers prepare for the profession, they take courses that give them a knowledge background. While that knowledge is useful, it reaches its full potential when it is not only implemented in the classroom *but also implemented well*. Even the best curriculum will be much less effective unless it is delivered with highly developed teaching skills.

Some argue that teachers and educators are synonymous. Others state that there is a difference. According to Sackstein (2016), the *Webster* definition of teacher is one whose occupation is to instruct whereby an educator is "one skilled in teaching." But for Sackstein, this distinction is not enough. For her "a teacher . . . is someone who shows up for a teaching job every day. He or she knows the content and likely sees teaching like a job, whereas an educator is one of those people who goes farther than what is expected. It is the teacher who makes relationships with students more important than the content, but because of those relationships, the content comes alive." To an educator, teaching is not just a job but a calling.

Most people perceive teaching as easy (Labaree, 2008); but teaching is highly complex. Consider what Fryshman (2014) says about the complexity of preparing teachers, as opposed to preparing candidates for other professions:

> Preparing a teacher is in a certain sense far more challenging than preparing other professionals. For all its variations, the physician's focus on the human body is limited. So is the building studied by the architect and the court of law facing the lawyer. The classroom awaiting the teacher, on the other hand, is almost infinite in its variations. [There are] hundreds or so language groups . . . [there is]

race, religion, sex, economic background, and age . . . variations in ability, in social problems—interest, physical and mental changes—the list is unending.

Every year our federal, state, and local governments spend billions of dollars on education, but this expenditure is wasted if effective teaching is not actually taking place at the grassroots level—in the classroom.

Over the past three decades, much research has been dedicated to determining what factors affect student achievement. One of the most significant studies conducted regarding what contributes most to student learning was led by William Sanders, a statistician at the University of Tennessee, and reported by Sanders and Rivers (1996).

Beginning in 1992, the state of Tennessee commissioned Dr. Sanders to analyze the teaching performance of its 30,000 teachers and the records of its six million students. In an interview conducted with Marks (2000), Dr. Sanders explained how he and his team examined class size; school location (rural, urban, suburban); ethnicity; students heterogeneously and homogeneously grouped; amount of expenditure per pupil; and percentage of students eligible for free lunch. Much to his surprise, he discovered that *teacher effectiveness* is 10–20 times as significant as any of these other effects. He was able to quantify just how much teachers matter and demonstrate that a "bad" teacher can deter the progress of a child for at least four years.

Wright, Horn, and Sanders (1997), in a subsequent study involving 60,000 students, came to the same conclusions. As a result, they recommended that the best way to improve education is to improve teacher effectiveness.

Sanders and his colleagues were not the only researchers to emphasize the importance of the teacher's performance on student achievement. Haycock (1998), working in Boston and Dallas, reported similar findings, with effective teachers having a profound influence.

The National Commission on Teaching and America's Future (1996) issued its influential report, which indicated that *what teachers know and can do is the most important influence on student learning*. Pipho (1998) concluded that the effectiveness of the individual classroom teacher was the single largest factor affecting student growth, with prior achievement, heterogeneity, and class size paling in comparison with actual teacher performance.

Nye, Konstantopoulos, and Hedges (2004) verified that what teachers do in the classroom has a direct effect on student achievement. Schneider (2015) reports research confirming that among in-school variables, it is the quality of the teacher that exerts the strongest influence on student success.

After studying in-service training and district innovations, Joyce and Showers (2002) determined that the key to the growth of students is the growth of teachers.

Despite increasing school safety, requiring uniforms, changing the curriculum, offering after-school programs, reducing class size, and increasing a lot more spending per pupil, Felch, Song, and Poindexter (2010) indicated that *the only progress that came in a chronically underperforming middle school was bringing in effective teachers.*

Hanushek (2011), in his own analysis, concluded that an effective teacher, which he defines as one in the top 15 percent for performance based on student achievement, can in one year take an average student from the 50th to the 58th percentile or above. The implication is that the same student with a teacher in the bottom 15 percent will end up below the 42nd percentile. And when assigned a teacher in the bottom 5 percent, a student in the middle of the distribution could fall to the bottom third by the end of the school year.

Hanushek's research also took into account student backgrounds and initial knowledge and applies to urban, suburban, and rural schools. He even goes on to calculate the economic impact of effective and ineffective teaching. Hanushek's study concluded that teachers in the top 15 percent (for performance based on student achievement) can add at least $20,000 of income *each year* throughout a student's life. In a class of 20 students, this teacher can add $400,000 *yearly* to the economy. On the other side of the coin, teachers in the lowest 15 percent can reduce this same amount *yearly* from the economy.

Economic and academic gains were not the only positive effects of excellent teaching. A study conducted with 2.5 million students over a 20-year period at Columbia and Harvard Universities demonstrated that effective teachers also had an effect on increasing college matriculation and reducing teenage pregnancies (Chetty, Friedman, & Rockoff, 2012).

If an effective teacher has the most significant influence on student learning as well as on other positive influences regardless of the background from which students come, then it is essential to understand what best teaching practices will have the most positive effect on students and how teachers can not only be constantly aware of these practices but also become proficient in improving them. This book is dedicated to identifying and developing the best teaching practices that will promote the success of all students.

Marie Menna Pagliaro

Introduction

Educational researcher Diane Ravitch (2003) provided evidence that pedagogical leaders have given credibility to dubious research findings *grounded more in ideology than in data.* In addition, she stated that unlike those in medicine who keep up with the latest medical research, educators do not exhibit the need to know the latest educational research.

A significant problem in improving teacher quality is getting an effective way to have teaching research reach practitioners (Tucker, 2016). Even when validated teaching practices that promote student learning are identified, few authorities require their evaluators to make accurate judgments that these practices are actually being implemented. The work of evaluators is reduced to assigning scores, which can be expressed as ratings, rankings, and numbers. Teaching evaluation is flawed when the complexity of teaching is transformed to judging behaviors that can be scored on a checklist, reducing teaching to numbers, rankings, and ratings (Danielson, 2016).

Wiener (2016) emphasizes the importance of assuring that those who evaluate teaching focus not on ratings but on how teachers can grow professionally. Concurrent with the problems of getting research to teachers and proving meaningful evaluation is finding a way to give effective feedback.

This book addresses the aforementioned issues. You will receive the most current research regarding teaching practice, obtain feedback with respect to your performance, and get information with respect to how you can improve. You will acquire new teaching skills related to student achievement and perfect those skills you already have. These goals will be achieved by using the Best Practices Observation Instruments (BPOIs) along with explicit directions with respect to how to use these instruments effectively.

There is a myriad of instructional skills. Marzano (2003a) synthesized them into three major categories verified by research—classroom curriculum design, instructional strategies, and classroom management.

These categories are covered in two books, which can be read in either order. This book, *Questioning, Instructional Strategies, and Classroom Management*, concentrates on best practices for developing classroom questioning (a skill involved in all instructions), using instructional strategies effectively, and becoming proficient at managing your classroom.

This book's companion text, *Designing and Implementing the Curriculum*, focuses on best practices in developing the school curriculum. Foundational areas integral to curriculum development include understanding and applying learning theory, emphasizing assessment and evaluation of learning, and constructing optimal units and lessons.

Since either book can be read first, the preface, introduction, and chapter 1 in both texts are the same. The preface delivers a framework for the book's importance. The first chapter provides the rationale for the BPOIs and an explanation regarding how to use these instruments to assess current practice in a relevant teaching area and then improve that practice.

It is likely that a vast majority of readers will already be practicing teachers. Therefore, instead of a detailed explanation of skills, a brief review will introduce the skills. This book would also be suitable for preservice teachers during methods courses and while student teaching and as such could also be an undergraduate text. Principals and assistant superintendents of instruction would find this text worthwhile in refreshing their own concepts of quality teaching and in helping their teachers deliver it.

To put the best practices skills criteria in context, these criteria will not appear as an isolated collection in themselves but *immediately* following each relevant review and update supporting the criteria.

Chapter 1

Becoming a Proficient Teacher

Learning even the most basic skills takes time, and developing teaching skills is a lifelong endeavor. A framework for acquiring teaching skills was offered by Joyce and Showers (1995, 2002). This framework includes theory exploration, demonstration, practice with accompanying feedback, and adaptation and generalization.

1. Theory exploration. As professionals, teachers must first understand the research that guides their practice. If you have completed a teacher-education program, you have already accomplished this knowledge and will accomplish more when you complete this text. You can further explore research through additional readings and discussions with colleagues.
2. Demonstration. In this phase, the skill to be improved or the new skill is modeled for the teacher. Examples of the skill in action may be conducted through written samples, a live demonstration by a peer, an outside expert, videotapes, or computer simulations. Teachers have often complained that in their teacher-education programs, professors never modeled or provided adequate examples of the practices that were promoted (Reiman & Thies-Sprinthall, 1998).
3. Practice with accompanying feedback. It has often been said that the three most important things in real estate are location, location, and location. It can also be said that the three most important activities in developing teaching skills are practice, practice, and practice.

The role of practicing cannot be overemphasized. Practice is required to develop any skill whether it is in the arts, sports, or teaching. You can do some of the practice on your own (unit planning, constructing teacher tests, rubric construction). But when your practice session involves interaction with students, it should be recorded through audio or videotaping so that performance is documented.

Though you can practice and evaluate your own performance, *practice is more effective when it occurs with colleagues.* Teaching used to be a very lonely profession. When a teacher closed his/her door, s/he had to fend for him/herself with no input from colleagues, only an occasional observation and checklist evaluation from a supervisor or principal.

As soon as possible after the practice session, you should receive feedback regarding your performance from your colleagues. Immediate feedback allows you to become aware of parts of your performance that were successful and those that needed adjustment. Receiving this feedback prevents poor performance from becoming routine.

When your performance is interactive in nature, microteaching, teaching a short lesson to a small group of your students, concentrating on only a few skills, usually not more than three, should be used. It is essential that the microteaching session be audio or videotaped.

Since a microteaching lesson is short and focuses on just a few skills, the teacher can specifically concentrate on developing just those particular skills and evaluating them readily. It is simple to count how many times they have appeared in the microteaching session so that subsequent microteaching sessions can document the increase of effective behaviors. Practice under microteaching conditions can then continue until the desired level of achievement has been realized.

4. Adaptation and generalization. There is no point in developing classroom skills if they are not actually implemented in the classroom. Once the skills have been practiced in a clinical setting with a small group of your peers or students, the skills can then be implemented with the whole class. Video or audiotaping interactive skills remains a critical necessity so that you can receive feedback for yourself and from your colleagues. In all cases, it is essential that you self-evaluate and self-reflect.

BEST PRACTICES OBSERVATION INSTRUMENTS

To address the issues of research-based practice, meaningful feedback, and evaluation for growth, you will be provided throughout this book with a collection of BPOIs. Each observation instrument (OI) cultivates a specific skill by offering a set of criteria for *developing* performance. The theory supporting each OI that follow was researched collaboratively by teachers, education professors, and teacher-education students. This theory is identified by the criteria listed in the OI for each best practices skill.

The BPOIs coach and guide your performance and document your growth. Documentation is of particular consequence because it has been reported historically that there is a gap in perception between what teachers think they do in the classroom and what they actually do (Delpit, 1995; Good & Brophy, 1974; Hook & Rosenshine, 1979; Sadker & Sadker, 1994).

The BPOIs offered will empower you to take control over your own development immediately.

HOW TO USE BPOIs

BPOIs are easy to complete. After experience with the first instrument, teachers have often expressed how simple these instruments are to work with and how effective they actually are in improving professional practice.

To illustrate how to use the BPOIs in this compendium, consider table 1.1, Best Practices for Professional Development. The criteria in this instrument, as well as those in all the instruments in this book, were developed by teachers, education professors, and education students after researching effective practices in professional development.

Table 1.1. Best Practices for Professional Development (T)

Criteria (Descriptors)	Performance Indicators (Examples)
The teacher identified reading for personal and professional broadening	identified *Classroom Instruction That Works* by Marzano, Pickering, and Pollock (2001)
read the materials and was able to describe what was learned	read text, learned that the nine major instructional strategies that affect student achievement are identifying similarities and differences; summarizing; reinforcing effort; homework and practice; using nonlinguistic representations, cooperative learning; setting objectives; generating and testing hypotheses; using questions, cues, and advance organizers
used the new learning acquired from the materials in the classroom	used similarities and differences when teaching verbs by comparing them with other verbs and contrasting them with other parts of speech
evaluated the effect of the new learning on instruction	evaluated students on subsequent test on which they performed significantly better than they had before I made the comparisons/contrasts and just gave them definitions and examples

(Continued)

Table 1.1.   (Continued)

Criteria (Descriptors)	Performance Indicators (Examples)
identified a relevant professional association (or associations)	identified the Association for Supervision and Curriculum Development (ASCD) identified the National Education Association (NEA)
joined the professional association(s)	joined ASCD in June
participated in the association's activities and can describe what was learned	
transferred the new learning acquired from the professional association to the classroom and evaluated the effect of the new learning	
identified a mentor to assist in professional development	identified veteran master teacher Marian Floyd
identified others with whom to network	identified and contacted June Larson and Roy Pinzer from neighboring districts
identified ways to act as an agent to arrange for complementing my teaching	
collaborated with colleagues to obtain feedback for self-reflection	collaborated with fellow fourth-grade teachers Lisa, Tom, and Frank
used guided observation for self-reflection	used the Best Practices for Lesson Planning OI with my colleagues to evaluate my video recording
sought input from learners	sought input from class every Friday in both writing and in classroom discussion regarding how well the week went and what could be done to improve instruction on the part of both the students and myself
used a self-reflective journal	used a self-reflective journal to jot down what happened each day. Arranged with Marian Floyd to discuss my journal once a week
developed a portfolio for self-reflection	
As a result of the above,	
identified own professional development needs	
devised a plan to meet the needs	
If learning a particular skill/model was identified as a need for development,	
explained the theory supporting the skill/model	

Criteria (Descriptors)	Performance Indicators (Examples)
If necessary,	
arranged to have the skill/model demonstrated by an expert or video simulation	
practiced the skill/model with feedback (under microteaching conditions where applicable) until a desired level of achievement was attained	
implemented that skill/model in the classroom	
evaluated the implementation of that skill/model in the classroom	
identified new areas for professional development	
discussed with colleagues if any changes (modifications, additions, deletions) were needed in the above criteria as a result of new research	

The instrument is filled in partially to explain how to use the remaining OIs in this book. Before you continue reading, examine this sample carefully. Viewing it will provide you with a frame of reference and a context for the explanation that follows.

You will notice that the OI is divided into two columns—Criteria (Descriptors) and Performance Indicators (Examples)—and that some of the Performance Indicators are completed and others are blank. The column on the left lists specific research-based skills (criteria), best practices associated with that particular skill.

The set of criteria on the left are specific and observable. Specificity and observability give the instrument reliability (Wiggins, 2005).

The criteria describe mastery performance. When working with BPOIs, you should understand from the beginning that it is not expected, necessary, or in most cases possible that anyone can perform all the criteria all the time (Wiggins, 1998). However, since the criteria are determined because they positively correlate with student achievement, implementing most of the criteria will increase the chances for reaching all learners successfully.

You will also note that the criteria are not *necessarily* listed in order. For instance, you can join a professional organization before identifying reading for personal broadening. You can identify peers with whom to work before doing either of the above. In some BPOIs that follow in this book, the order will be important; in others it will not.

The column on the right presents the Performance Indicators. The teacher (colleagues/evaluators) must put in writing in this column *exactly* how each criterion was actually demonstrated, providing clear, detailed, and appropriate examples. This process provides objective and more reliable performance data, making it easier for several observers (peers/colleagues) to agree that the performance has actually occurred.

Documentation of the examples is more focused and precise because the same verb and tense stated in the criterion are also used in the indicator. Verbs used in the Criteria (Descriptors) are expressed in the past tense describing what the teacher actually did, not what s/he plans to do.

For instance, the third criterion in the Best Practices for Professional Development OI is, "Enlisted peers with whom to collaborate." Inappropriate ways to state the Performance Indicator would be stating what will be done in that category; putting a check, writing "Satisfied," "Completed," "Yes," or an equivalent term next to the corresponding criterion; numerically scoring the criterion; or offering an irrelevant example. Appropriate ways of stating the Performance Indicator for the above would be writing the names of the persons who agreed to be collaborators next to the corresponding criterion such as, "Enlisted (same verb and tense as the one in criterion) Paul and Sally from my teaching team." Otherwise, the Performance Indicator for this criterion would remain blank.

Because the documentation is so specific, the BPOIs are more informative than the traditional type of instrument that judges performance through rating scales where raters place a check mark for each criterion in the corresponding box. Traditional OIs, with scale variations (1–4, 1–5, 1–7), are commonly used to evaluate teachers. However, these OIs "don't give specific enough information . . . to use for further learning" (Brookhart, 2004, p. 77). Receiving a reported rating (score), such as 3 for Average on any scale used does give some feedback. But this rating is useless in helping a teacher grow because it neither informs the teacher during the self-reflective process what "Average" performance actually is nor guides him/her how to improve in that category.

You have already observed that there are blank spaces under Performance Indicators in the Best Practices for Professional Development OI presented previously. Spaces that are not filled provide specific feedback identifying where performance could be improved. Table 1.2 shows how to complete the performance indicators.

The first session using these instruments provides baseline data regarding performance on that skill. From the baseline data, it can then be determined which additional criteria (descriptors) should be demonstrated or increased and which ineffective criteria demonstrated, if any are identified as such on an instrument, should be avoided in future performance. After obtaining the baseline data, the teacher can then practice, addressing only a few criteria at one time.

In their attempt to offer a teacher evaluation system that goes beyond using observation forms and changing them periodically, Danielson and McGreal

(2000) have offered a blueprint with three essential attributes: the "what," the "how," and "trained evaluators."

The "what" includes clear criteria for exemplary practice based on current research; the "how" involves the ability of school districts to guarantee that teachers can demonstrate the criteria; and "trained evaluators" who can assure that regardless of who is conducting the evaluation, the judgment is consistent and, therefore, reliable.

The BPOIs fulfill all three criteria suggested by Danielson and McGreal (2000). These instruments express criteria for mastery performance (best practices), help teachers demonstrate criteria by indicating which have and which have not been evidenced by appropriate examples, thereby identifying areas needed for practice, and provide a forum for "reliable evaluations" where the teacher him/herself must indicate and peer evaluators must agree which specific and accurate examples of criteria were implemented during actual performance.

Moreover, in the discussions of the examples among all participants, suggestions can be offered for *better* examples that could have been implemented. This interaction is professionalism at its best because it is highly effective in improving instruction and growth for all participants (Danielson, 2007). "Watching teachers in action, using systematic, validated observational approaches, allows trained observers to see very clearly what good teachers do to foster learning" (Pianta, 2007, p. 11). The OIs assist teachers and their colleague observers to ensure that agreed-upon researched criteria correlated with student achievement are understood and actually implemented in the classroom.

Using the BPOIs, you are now prepared to apply the framework for acquiring teaching skills (Joyce & Showers, 1995, 2002) introduced earlier in this chapter: theory exploration, demonstration, practice with feedback, and adaptation and generalization. You should understand why the criteria in the OI are essential (theory exploration).

Familiarity with the research and discussion with peers are crucial processes in assisting participants in both identifying and then internalizing the

Table 1.2. Completing Performance Indicators for Corresponding Best Practices Criteria

Correct Completion	Incorrect Completion
Use the same verb.	Use a different verb.
Use the same tense.	Write what will be done.
Provide a *specific detailed* example.	Provide a general or vague example.
Provide a relevant example.	Provide an irrelevant example
Provide any additional examples that may have been performed for the same criterion.	Use terms such as "Yes," "Completed," or "Satisfied." Place a check mark. Score numerically.

criteria. If there is a question about any criterion that is not clear, an example of the criterion should be provided (demonstration).

Practicing using the OI can then follow in a controlled environment. You may recall the old adage that practice makes perfect. Wolfe (2001) reminded teachers that practice also makes permanent.

As previously stated, microteaching can be conducted with a small group of your students. If you and your colleagues are satisfied with your performance, you can then implement the new skills with your entire class (adaptation and generalization).

Some BPOIs, such as one that may be developed for lesson planning, have criteria that can be demonstrated within a class period. Other OIs take a longer time to implement, such as the Professional Development instrument offered earlier and the implementation of the Best Practices for Unit Planning OI. OIs that take a longer time to implement are coded (T).

Above all, it must be clear that BPOIs are *dynamic*. These living documents are works in progress, guidelines whose criteria should be modified when new research develops. As more studies reveal different criteria for performance excellence and as new and validated strategies and criteria are proposed, collaborators should revise these BPOIs and/or develop new ones.

Also, it is essential to understand that a teacher can demonstrate all the criteria in the OIs and yet be ineffective. The reason is that teaching is more than the sum of its parts. There are always intangibles involved that can contribute to effective or ineffective performance.

BPOIs empower teachers to take control over their performance with constant reminders regarding mastery performance, what they actually performed, and what they could yet perform.

In conclusion, BPOIs

- expose teachers to best practices;
- offer a medium in which to internalize best practices;
- analyze present teaching performance;
- compare present performance to best practices by identifying skills yet to be implemented;
- serve as tools for acquiring new repertoires of strategies;
- foster communication and dialog among colleagues to continually identify excellent teaching criteria;
- provide a forum for discussing with colleagues more effective examples of criteria that could have been implemented;
- provide a structure for adjusting criteria and for creating new instruments when a new strategy and/or new research emerges; and
- evaluate the implementation of the strategy after practice.

Chapter 2

Developing Proficient Questioning Skills

REVIEW AND UPDATE

Researchers have consistently reported that questioning is one of the teaching skills having the greatest effect on student achievement (Danielson, 1996, 2008; Good, 1996; Interstate New Teacher Assessment and Support Consortium [INTASC], 1995; Wang, Haertel, & Walberg, 1993). Therefore, considerable attention should be given to developing the questioning skills of both novice and veteran teachers.

At the core of all learning is the ability to ask questions. While classroom questioning originally focused on having students acquire specific knowledge, more recently there has been a shift toward using questions to promote and enhance learning. In addition to learning academic subjects, students must learn to deal with an ever-changing world by using questions to handle their own lives analytically and intelligently.

Treffinger (2008) challenges teachers to reflect on the current everyday experiences of children and teenagers. They can communicate through images, videos, or by simply speaking with young people all over the world. Our students have access to more technology than that in the workplaces of their parents two decades ago. Currently, students are studying new subjects that did not exist only a few years ago and will prepare for careers that are not in existence today. It is becoming increasingly common for our students to interact with people of diverse backgrounds and collaborate with people all over the planet. With all of these with which to deal and with the increasing unknowns in the world, students will need the tools to become effective creative and critical thinkers. And for these kinds of thinking, questioning is an essential tool.

Questioning is fundamental to investigating systematically *all curriculum areas*. In the pursuit of this investigation, students must question the reason(s) for the inquiry, make use of questions to guide the search for information, integrate the results, and employ questions to evaluate these results.

Teachers play a critical role in questioning. It is, therefore, incumbent upon you to plan questions very carefully so that student knowledge and comprehension will be enhanced. The quality of the question determines the depth of student understanding. Moreover, teachers are models in the questioning process for their students. Therefore, high quality of a teacher's questioning should facilitate the student's ability to ask questions and think independently.

ESTABLISHING AN EFFECTIVE ENVIRONMENT FOR QUESTIONING

Before embarking on a discussion of questioning, it must be emphasized that all questions involve content. The teacher must master the content if s/he is to develop an environment for effective questioning skills. The more a teacher knows about the content, the better the questions the teacher has the potential to ask, especially those that lead students to deeper meaning and critical thinking.

When analyzing questioning, it is useful to point out that there is a distinction between the skill of formulating the original question itself and how skillfully the teacher reacts to a student's response. A teacher may have an excellent idea for a question but may not phrase and/or distribute it well or handle appropriately an answer a student may give. Therefore, the question itself loses its effectiveness. It is also a given that the vocabulary the teacher uses in questions must be consistent with the vocabulary parameters of the students.

Questions do not occur in isolation. For both teacher and student questioning to be effective, it must be implemented in a supportive learning environment. In this environment, the teacher is a facilitator who fosters not only students' academic growth but also their personal and social growth. The classroom is a learning community in which there is shared responsibility for the success of all community members. The teacher's role is one of a guide and coach as opposed to a person who pours information into students' heads. There is a warm, friendly atmosphere where all members show mutual respect for and support each other in a spirit of cooperation in which all have a stake in the success of all other members. This atmosphere produces a *comfort level* in which students are more willing to take risks in answering and asking questions to enhance achievement.

Recently, several characteristics have been demonstrated to be conducive to promoting a positive emotional classroom environment for questioning. These involve having a caring attitude, setting high standards, and having *all* classroom members, including the teacher, show mutual respect and support for each other (Oakes & Lipton, 2003). In short, there is a sense of community in the class where all classroom members are connected with one another. Research has indicated that rapport with the teacher and fellow classmates made students feel connected and willing to participate, thus enhancing cognitive and affective learning (Frisby & Martin, 2010).

This supportive learning environment welcomes student questions, is nonjudgmental, fosters the attitude that it is all right to make mistakes because we all do and learn from them, and does not allow students to be subjected to ridicule from anyone in the learning community. Students are given the time to think and are challenged at their appropriate levels.

The seating arrangement in the classroom is critically important for effective questioning. Whenever possible, students should sit in a circle where they all face each other and can address each other in a more personal way. In this setting, all students are easily visible to the teacher and to each other, with little opportunity for students to conduct nonrelated activities. The teacher is free to move around, thus giving him/her contact with everyone in the class.

In a supportive learning environment, the teacher is enthusiastic and plans a dynamic curriculum. S/he expects all to participate by framing questions thoughtfully and by assisting with the help of the rest of the class any student who does not know an answer or who does not complete a full response.

Once you have established this supportive learning environment with your students, you will be well on your way to implementing questioning (and your entire curriculum) more effectively.

Characteristics of an Effective Questioning Environment

- Teacher knowledgeable in subject matter
- Teacher as a facilitator
- Mutual caring
- Mutual respect
- Mutual support
- Shared responsibility for success of all
- Success of one critical to success of all
- Feeling of connectedness
- Nonjudgmental attitude
- High comfort level

From your own school experience, you will recall that most classroom time is spent in verbal interaction (questioning), largely between teachers and students. In fact, researchers have reported that questioning is the second most common method used in instruction after lecturing (Black, 2001). Of this verbal interaction, 80 percent involves questions by teachers and answers by students, and that teachers, both elementary and secondary, ask as many as 100 questions per hour (Borich, 2007). Similar results are reported by Vogler (2008), with teachers asking 300–400 questions per day and up to 120 questions per hour.

Since so much classroom time is devoted to questioning, and research has identified a strong correlation between the teacher's effective questioning skills and student test performance (Cotton, 2000; Marzano et al., 2001), it is vital that questioning be implemented well. Questioning is an essential learning tool and *one of the most complex skills for teachers, even experienced teachers, to master.* To add to the complexity, different types of questions are appropriate for different types of instructional strategies.

Though it is difficult even for veteran teachers to demonstrate excellent questioning skills, it is important that you *practice* doing so because student achievement is at stake. Once you master these skills, you will immediately notice a positive difference in your students, a smoother flow of interactions, and more dynamic relationships in your classroom. You will even notice fewer discipline problems.

EFFECTIVE QUESTIONING PRACTICES WHEN FRAMING AND DELIVERING QUESTIONS

The most important reason for studying questioning skills is to learn how to actively involve your students in acquiring, exploring, and manipulating meaningful information (Weiss & Pasley, 2004). This type of questioning creates a powerful learning environment.

Classroom questioning usually follows a series of phases (Dillon, 1988).

These phases will serve as a framework for analyzing effective and ineffective questioning practices.

After structuring a topic with a statement,

Phase 1. the teacher frames a question and delivers it to one or more students;
Phase 2. the student(s) provide(s) a response; and
Phase 3. the teacher reacts to that response.

Only phases 1 and 3 involve teacher behavior. In the following section, you will examine each of these two phases separately to review which teacher questioning behaviors implemented or avoided will have the most positive effects on students. It is important to state that regardless of the ways questions are framed, delivered, and reacted to, a teacher who proceeds through all phases with interest, enthusiasm, and a conversational tone is highly likely to get these same characteristics from students.

Phase 1: The Teacher Asks a Question and Addresses It to One or More Students

Secure the attention of the class before asking a question

Before asking a question, make sure you have everyone's attention. If students are not listening, not paying attention, then why ask a question or conduct any kind of instruction? Brain research informs us that attention is necessary for memory and, therefore, to all learning (Jensen, 1998).

When asking questions, some teachers talk above students' voices. This teacher behavior conveys a subtle message that the question (or lesson) is unimportant and, therefore, not worthy of the students' attention.

Keep lower-level questions to a minimum

Ever since the first reported study on questioning was conducted (Stevens, 1912) through more recent times (Wilen, 2001; Wragg, 1993; Wragg & Brown, 2001), it has been noted that a vast majority of questions asked by teachers are low level. Moreover, these low-level questions are predominantly asked from the elementary school through the university levels (Albergaria-Almeida, 2010).

Low-level questions are referred to in the educational literature as fact, closed, or *convergent* questions. They lead to simple recall and limited responses and are usually either right or wrong.

Because some questions are on the memory level, however, does not mean they are not important. Memory matters and is a crucial foundation for all learning and higher thinking levels. Memory (lower cognitive) questions become problematic when they are a vast majority of the questions asked, especially with students whose developmental stage makes it possible for them to learn and grow at a higher level. Research indicates that lower cognitive questions are more effective with young children when the purpose is the mastery of basic skills; higher cognitive questions yield superior learning gains for older primary, middle, and secondary students (Gall, Gall, & Borg, 2003).

Higher-level questions are referred to in the educational literature as *divergent* or open questions. These questions require longer responses from students by requiring students to manipulate facts and use higher levels of thinking. The students do more of the talking, and the teacher eventually ends up asking *fewer* questions (Chuska, 1995). Whoever is doing the talking is doing the work, and whoever is doing the work is doing the learning (Wong, 1989). When the quality of the teacher's question elicits a higher cognitive response from the student, student talk is increased.

Divergent (open) questions lead to higher-level thinking and longer responses and can have several correct answers. These thought-provoking questions make instruction more student-centered.

You should be aware that questions beginning with who, when, and where are generally fact questions. Questions beginning with how, why, or what may be either fact or thought questions depending upon what follows.

Some teachers deliberately plan their questions so that they will be predominantly high-level. To accomplish this, these teachers use Bloom's taxonomy (knowledge, comprehension, application, synthesis, and evaluation) as a guide. An alternative hierarchy includes retrieval, analytical, predictive, and interpretive questions (Marzano, 2017).

Phrase questions for clarity

Consider the following question: "What about Cuba?"

Your reaction probably is, "Well, what about it?" You do not have a clear idea regarding what information is being asked. Now consider the question rephrased: "How is the climate of Cuba related to its economy?" This second question gives you a focus and helps you retrieve and coordinate the information needed to respond.

Another type of vague question is, "Tell us about triangles." You are likely asking yourself what you are being asked about triangles.

To assure that questions are clear, they should be narrowed down and not so wordy that students lose track of the information requested. Key questions should be related to the lesson objective and planned in advance to provide clarity so that there is no need to rephrase questions during the lesson. Writing key questions to which you can refer helps both beginning and experienced teachers keep the lesson on target.

After you write your questions, read them *out loud*. Actually hearing them will give you a better handle on how they are coming across. If necessary, adjust the questions.

Then, based on the original question, consider possible additional questions that would lead students to deeper understanding of the concepts presented and promote further investigation.

Develop key questions sequentially

Set the stage by asking beginning questions with basic or known content. Subsequent pivotal questions should be planned carefully, presented logically, and asked in sequential order. Planning, writing, and asking questions in sequence also assist students in developing a deeper understanding of information and the opportunity to apply it.

It is crucial to point out that so much can occur spontaneously or serendipitously in the classroom that there may be occasions when pursuing the unexpected instead of what was planned may lead to clarification and/or deeper knowledge and understanding. This principle holds true for planned lessons, as well as for planned questions.

Keep the speed of your question (and speech in general) appropriate to the age level of your students

Recent research has reported that adults speak at an average rate of 170 words per minute (Tobias, 2008). It takes students a longer time to process questions and information in general, with the average five-to-seven-year-olds processing speech at the rate of only 120 words per minute and the average student in high school processing speech at the rate of 140–145 words per minute. In *both* cases, the processing rate is considerably less than that of the speaking rate of adults. Therefore, if you want students to listen so that they really hear and understand, speak at a rate that is compatible with their processing level.

Increase wait-time (pausing)

A common teacher practice in many classrooms is that of rapid-fire questioning. In this type of classroom, the teacher asks a question, immediately calls on a student for a response, immediately reacts to the student's response, and immediately asks another question, thus repeating the same cycle. Though waiting long enough for a student to respond seems to be a relatively simple behavior, *it is one that teachers have difficulty putting into practice*. In general, teachers have little tolerance for silence and may even feel that when there is silence in the classroom, they are losing control.

Rowe (1974) trained teachers to increase time after soliciting a question from students, which she calls *wait-time 1*, by pausing from three to five seconds. She found that when teachers waited this amount of time, student responses improved in the following ways:

1. The length of the response increases.
2. The number of unsolicited but appropriate responses increases.
3. Failure to respond decreases.
4. Confidence, as reflected in decrease of inflected (question-like tones of voice) responses, increases.
5. Incidence of speculative responses increases.
6. Incidence of child-child comparisons of data increases.
7. Incidence of evidence-inference statements increases.

8. Incidence of student questions increases.
9. Incidence of responses from students rated by teachers as relatively slow increases.
10. Variety in types of moves made by students increases (Rowe, 1974, p. 81).

Rowe (1986) subsequently reported that pausing (increasing wait-time 1) changed the discussion from an "inquisitional" nature where *teachers* do most of the structuring and soliciting, and students do the responding, to a more "conversational" nature where *both* the teacher and the students engage in structuring, soliciting, and responding.

To improve the responses of your pupils, you should pause at least three to five seconds after asking a question and selecting a student to answer. If after asking questions, you find yourself not pausing long enough before calling on respondents and subsequently decide to increase your wait-time, it would be productive to *prepare the respondents* by informing them of your intent and the reasons for it. Your students will also have to adjust to your new behavior.

Ask only one question at a time

What is your reaction to the question, "Where is the liver and what does it do for your body?" You probably do not know which part of the question to think about or answer first. This type of question is often labeled a double question. Asking this type of question is confusing and distracts students from their ability to respond in a way that assists you in assessing their learning.

Ask your question before you call on a student to respond

Picture yourself in the following classroom where a teacher could ask a question in either of these two ways. What do you think would be the result in each case?

"Henrietta, how could you improve this sentence?"

"How could you improve this sentence?" (Pause) "Henrietta."

Chances are that in phrasing the first question mentioned previously, only Henrietta is alerted to concentrate on an answer. In the second question, all students are alerted, and many are likely to volunteer by raising their hands before the teacher calls on Henrietta.

Always be sure to call on one specific student to respond, and make sure that you *call on that student by name*. If you allow students to call out, it will lead to chaos. Also, calling out provides the opportunity for those who do not want to pay attention and participate in class to let others take over.

Gear your questions to the ability levels of the students

Your goal is to have meaningful participation from *all* students to ensure their success. To accomplish this goal, you have to address the learning needs of diverse students. For example, big picture questions could be directed to holistic learners and detail questions to sequential learners. More space and time could be given to introverts who prefer listening and absorbing information and may be better able to answer summarizing questions.

Call on students when you are confident that they will be able to answer correctly by targeting their ability, interest, and readiness level. This *may* mean that at times you will address less demanding questions to some and more demanding questions to others while expecting high achievement from all. Your ultimate objective should require all to consider essential under-standings at high cognitive levels but at varying degrees of difficulty so that all your students are challenged.

However, since students rise to the expectation of the teacher, it is imperative that you give low-achieving students, when they make an error in responding, the same probing that you would give high-achieving students, when they answer incorrectly. You could respond to errors or incomplete answers of low-achieving students by informing them what is correct and incorrect in the answer. You could advise that student that you will return to him/her after there is more time to consider the response *and then do so*. Or present students with the high-level question in advance, and allow them to rehearse the answer with a partner (Marzano, 2017).

What is most important in whatever you choose to do is that your behavior informs low-achieving students that they are expected to be challenged and perform at high levels.

Distribute your questions so that everyone has a chance to participate

You will want all students to feel as though they are part of your instruction and that their input is important. Keep your antennae out so that you are aware of who has and who has not had the opportunity to respond, and call on everyone at least once. Frequently scan the room to determine not only who has not responded but also who may be confused, irritated, or who may lack interest. Remind students that you care about their participation because *the more they participate, the more they achieve.*

During your questioning, you will want to keep students engaged. So even after answering a question, a student should not feel that his/her participation has ended. You can keep students involved in a discussion through calling on students randomly, requesting responses through hand signals, having stu-dents discuss their answers in pairs, or calling on a second student to explain the prior answer of a first student (Marzano, 2017).

Be aware of the fact that teachers tend to treat boys and girls differently in schools (American Association of University Women, 1992; Sadker & Sadker, 1994, 1997). You should be aware of the results of the research so that you will implement instruction in your class in which boys and girls have equal expectations and opportunities for success. The research cited earlier has reported that girls were more frequently underchallenged and that *both male and female teachers* in general tended to treat boys and girls differently. According to Sadker and Sadker (1994), during questioning, boys are:

- encouraged more than girls;
- called on more often;
- asked more higher-level questions;
- given more reinforcement for their responses, whether correct or not; and
- probed more often for their responses.

On the other side of the coin, it should be noted that other studies found that boys are subject to greater inequities than girls in schools (Sommers, 1996) and that in some situations, girls are given preferential treatment and, in other situations, boys are given preferences (Lee, Chen, & Smerdon, 1996).

As far as you are concerned, it is your responsibility to be cognizant of the tendency for treating boys and girls inequitably in different situations and to ensure that during your questioning as well as in all other instructional activities, you avoid any gender bias in your own classroom.

In some situations, it would be beneficial to have students answer in full sentences and/or to *write* their responses to questions. When answering in a full sentence, the students must listen to the question, process it, and then integrate the question and answer into a complete thought. This integration may help improve composition-writing skills. For some students, writing answers instead of responding orally could provide a better opportunity for participation. This process could be especially productive for English language learners, who should be expected to participate, though they may need more time and support to answer the original question and subsequent assistance with the response.

Call on both volunteers and nonvolunteers

To avoid the possibility that a few students will dominate the discussion, leaving the rest of the class frustrated (or relieved), call on both volunteers and nonvolunteers. Calling on volunteers encourages them to keep participating. Calling on the nonvolunteers tells them that they are *expected* to participate. When students do not know when they will be called on to answer a question or give feedback on the previous student's answer, there is an increase in their attention to your questions and to their classmates' responses.

However, calling on nonvolunteers must be conducted in a nonthreatening way. Improper teacher body language and/or verbal tone that communicate impatience or annoyance can turn nonvolunteers off and further discourage them from volunteering or actually responding.

Personalize questions

Whenever appropriate, use the pronoun "you." Students feel more connected and are more motivated when you ask questions such as, "If *you* were in this situation, what would *you* do?" or "Pretend that *you* are Jim. How would *you* react to his brother?"

Use a collaborative approach

Situations may occur in which everyone's input on a topic or problem would be helpful. It gives everyone a feeling that s/he is part of a solution. These situations could be managerial or academic. Some examples include:

"How could *we* line up so that everyone can be dismissed safely and quickly?"
"How can *we* solve this triangle problem?"
"How can *we* help each other eat a healthier diet?"

INEFFECTIVE CLASSROOM QUESTIONING PRACTICES WHEN FRAMING AND DELIVERING QUESTIONS

From your own experience, you should be aware of how complex the effective phrasing and delivery of questions can actually be. Skill in achieving both can significantly increase student participation and achievement. To ensure that this process is as smooth and productive as possible, you should avoid several ineffective framing and delivery questioning behaviors.

Repeating or Rephrasing Questions Immediately After Asking Them

If you have carefully thought through the pivotal questions for the lesson, and have secured the students' attention before asking questions, there should be no need to repeat or rephrase them. Yet, repeating questions is a common teacher behavior. Repeating questions wastes time. Moreover, if the students know that you will repeat the question, they will tend not to listen the first time.

Asking and Answering Your Own Questions

When teachers do not get an immediate response, they sometimes find themselves answering their own questions. This practice defeats the purpose of asking the question in the first place.

You may want to determine why the students may not be responding. Is the question vague? Is it confusing? Do the students have the informational or experiential readiness to answer the question? Assuming that the students do have the background to answer the question and that you have framed it properly, you can avoid answering the question yourself by approaching the content from a different perspective, by asking a series of developmental questions that will help the students respond, or by asking the students why they are having difficulty responding.

Asking Questions Which Require a Chorus Response

When students are asked to respond all together, it leads to calling out and to rewarding those who do not wish to participate. Allowing calling out provides a fertile environment for a few to dominate the class and for an unruly atmosphere that can lead to behavior problems.

However, when students are unsure of a generalization or rule, it would be acceptable to reinforce the content through a chorus response once basic information is understood.

Example:

Ms. Johnson has listed the following *ei* and *ie* words on the board in two columns (Table 2.1). The *ei* and *ie* in each word are underlined in colored chalk.

Ms. Johnson asks the class if they see any pattern in the *ei* words listed in the A column that is different from the *ie* words. The students should be able to see that the letter *c* precedes the *ei* words. After they observe this, Ms. Johnson states the rule, "*i* before *e* except after *c*." Ms. Johnson then asks the class to repeat the rule in unison several times. While they state the rule, she points to the *ei* and then *c*, demonstrating or having a student demonstrate what the class is stating.

Asking Questions Requiring Yes-No Answers

Questions requiring yes-no answers give students a 50–50 chance of getting the correct answer. Therefore, the answer does not necessarily give the teacher insights regarding the students' knowledge. Questions that lead to yes-no responses are not higher-level questions and require only factual information.

Another type of yes-no question is, "Does everybody understand?" This question is, unfortunately, asked too frequently. What teachers really tell their students when asking this question is that this is their last chance so that if they

Table 2.1. Spelling *ei* and *ie* Words

Column A- ei *Words*	*Column B-* ie *Words*
receive	retrieve
conceive	believe
perceive	brief

don't ask any questions, then this means that the students understand completely, freeing the teacher to move on. The problem is that sometimes students do not understand that they do not understand, and if they do not know what they do not know, there is no way that they can ask a question about it.

Asking Questions Requiring One-Word Answers

As in the case of questions requiring yes-no answers, questions requiring one-word responses elicit only factual information and do not develop the cognitive abilities of students. Though these questions may serve some function in a discussion, such as assuring foundational information or transitioning from one topic to the next, they should be held to a minimum.

Asking Leading Questions

Leading questions are the type that restrict students' thinking by limiting their responses and, therefore, do not provide the teacher with accurate feedback regarding student achievement.

There are three types of leading questions:

a. rhetorical questions;
b. those that contain part of the answer in the question; and
c. those that assume the answer in the question.

  a. Rhetorical questions are not questions per se but statements posed as questions. In effect, these questions are not actually expected to be answered. Rhetorical questions are often intended to have the students agree with the teacher, which is usually yes. If the students do not literally say yes, they will think it. (Once they agree, they will likely also agree with what follows.) Rhetorical questions are also sometimes used when a teacher hedges, wanting to make a statement but not confident enough to assert a point.
  b. Questions that contain part of the answer in the question or supply part of the answer to complete the question are ineffective in determining student knowledge.
  Suppose someone said to you, "Leonardo di _____." You would probably say Caprio (or if you heard da instead of di, you might say Vinci). You have already provided a response; but has anyone asked you a question? Sometimes, teachers phrase questions in a way that includes part of the answer: "The hero in the movie, Titanic, is Leonardo di . . ." Whether the student knows the correct answer or not, s/he is able to supply an answer.
  c. Other types of leading questions propose that something is true by hiding it in a question. These questions are structured to guide a person to think in a certain way.

One type solicits agreement, forcing a yes or no response. "Don't you agree that this is an appropriate book for teenagers?" is the type of leading question that implies a student should agree. It would be more effective to say, "Explain why you think that this is or is not an appropriate book for teenagers."

"Isn't that all right?" is another example. This question does not allow for students to respond if they think that something is not all right.

"Why did he make the correct decision?" is a question that does not leave room for students to disagree with the decision. Better worded, the question would read, "What conditions would have made you come to this decision or to a different one?"

To summarize, leading questions force students to agree with the question and do not foster them to think independently.

Unprofessional Phrasing

Teachers should avoid phrasing questions as direct statements that end up as questions. "The function of the gall bladder is what?" "The gall bladder is located where?" These "questions" should be phrased: "What is the function of the gall bladder?" and "Where is the gall bladder located?"

Clumsy wording also occurs when the teacher asks questions that end in prepositions. Note how much smoother the phrasing of the second question is in the following two examples:

"Which flask should this solution be poured into?"
"Into which flask should we pour this solution?"
Other unprofessionally worded questions are: "Who knows . . .?" "Who can tell the class . . .?" or "Does anyone know . . .?" It is more effective to ask the question, pause, and then call on a student to respond.

EFFECTIVE QUESTIONING PRACTICES WHEN RESPONDING TO A STUDENT'S ANSWER

You will recall that after a teacher poses and delivers a question in Phase 1, the student provides a response in Phase 2. Students may respond in any of the following ways:

Provide no response
Refuse to answer

State they do not know
Provide the correct response
Offer a partially correct response
Provide an incorrect response
State they did not hear the question
Offer an unexpected response
Answer in a silly way
Call out
Ask a related or different question

During the time that a student responds (or does not respond), you must be a careful listener and observer. You need also to be aware of the reasons that some students may be hesitant to respond to your question(s). Among these reasons are your expectation of an immediate response, not knowing the answer or having difficulty expressing it, not being sure of the question as expressed, anxiety regarding failure or ridicule, apathy, and general fear of expressing responses publicly. All of these will be diminished if you have taken the time, as indicated in the beginning of this chapter, to structure a positive and supportive classroom environment.

If a student does choose to respond, the content may be influenced by his/her past experience with success or failure; age; culture; past experience with similar situations involved in the question; peer beliefs; personal values, biases, and beliefs; or prior learning (Chuska, 1995).

Occasionally, a student may respond by asking a question. If this should occur, ask the class how *they* would answer the question instead of immediately answering it yourself.

At this point, it must be emphasized that you should train students to answer in a tone that can be *heard* by the entire class. Reticent students and those who are unsure will tend to speak more softly and, perhaps, even inaudibly. Yet, these students should understand that their input is important and that everyone wants to share in that input, regardless of what the student presently knows, because the goal of a supportive class is to have everyone feel comfortable and achieve.

It ought to be noted that you should not interrupt a student who is trying to respond, especially when that student is making a sincere effort. This student needs time and patience from the entire classroom community.

EFFECTIVE RESPONSES TO STUDENTS' ANSWERS

There is so much spontaneity that occurs in classrooms and no set formulas that teachers can follow to react to students' responses. Questioning is not only a skill but also an art. Most questioning and responding require that teachers think on their feet. However, there are some techniques teachers can use to keep their talking to a minimum while keeping students involved and promoting higher-level thinking. Here the quality of teacher feedback will determine how student knowledge will be enhanced.

Positive (effective) questioning in Phase 3 includes the following practices.

Increasing Wait-Time 2

Frequently, teachers are so quick to respond to a student's answer, less than one second, that they do not give themselves enough time to consider the answer, come up with a cogent reaction, and provide enough time for the responding student to complete his/her thought, for other students to respond to the same question, or for students to react to each other's answers. You have already reviewed wait-time 1, the time between the teacher asking a question and calling on a student to respond. Wait-time 2 is the time between a student's answer and the teacher's resumption of speaking. Increasing wait-time 2 to at least three seconds before providing feedback, cueing, probing, or redirecting has been positively correlated with student achievement (White & Tisher, 1986). Here again, as in wait-time 1, if you have not been taking the time to respond to students' answers, inform the class that you will be taking this time and the reasons for it.

Give Some Feedback to a Student's Answer

It is generally agreed that some feedback should be given to a student's answer. "Feedback provides immediacy and impact to an activity" (Good & Brophy, 1997, p. 229). No feedback given to a student's response, *even if the answer is correct*, is often perceived as negative feedback. You should also note that students would rather know their answer was incorrect (receive negative feedback) than have no knowledge of results at all.

Brophy (1979) concluded that the attributes of effective feedback are:

Honesty. If you praise a student for an incorrect response, your praise will eventually be ignored by all students. Accepting an incorrect response just to make a student feel good does not extend his/her ability to achieve.
Contingency. Answers that are correct should be praised; answers that are incorrect should be corrected.
Specificity. Students should know exactly what deserves praise ("You answered that question on a very mature level.") and what needs correction ("Check the past participles on the irregular verb list I distributed.").

Teacher's praise for a student's answer can be given *when warranted* by changing the mode of response so that it does not become boring and ineffectual. "Good," "Great," "Super," "Good thinking," "Great insight," "Fine job," and "Never thought of that myself" are just a few of the responses you can give students.

It should be pointed out that some educators believe that praise can be problematic (Kohn, 2001; Tauber, 2007). They see praise as manipulative, something teachers do to force students to cooperate. Praise may increase students' dependence on the teacher instead of having students participating for their own sake. However, Dreikurs (1998) promoted the practice of praising *effort* rather than performance because effort is within the student's control whereas innate ability that could lead to higher performance levels is not.

Recent research has concluded that praise is linked to the difference in perception between how students view their intelligence—those who view their intelligence as fixed and those who believe that intelligence can be improved through effort. Praise for intelligence tends to lead students to a fixed mind-set, resulting in a lack of motivation and resilience; praise for effort is more conducive to developing a growth mind-set, which fosters working hard (Dweck, 2008). She recommends "process" praise (feedback) for involvement, perseverance, and growth, which all nurture robust motivation. Process praise informs students what they have performed in order to achieve success and what they can do to repeat that success.

Examples of process praise teachers can use in response to what effort students have made to answer questions are the following:

"Wow! You really thought through that answer. It showed how you were able to go back and put together what you already knew. Congratulations."
"That was a tough question, but you stayed with it until you integrated so many different ideas. Kudos."
"Putting that answer together took a lot of thinking. It showed how your effort led us all see the situation much clearer. Thanks."

In Phase 3 (the teacher responds to the student's answer), the most appropriate teacher feedback comes in reaction to *specific* responses of students.

If a Student Did Not Hear the Question, Ask Another Student to Repeat It

This teacher response conveys a subliminal message that the student called on should have been listening in the first place. Of course, this teacher response assumes that s/he had everyone's attention before asking the question.

Encourage Sustained Responses from Students

It has been reported that encouraging student responses so that they express their own ideas, personal opinions, experiences, and understandings makes the class more student-centered. Correspondingly, students' answers are longer and more articulate and reflect a higher level of thinking (Oliveira, 2010). This effect is evidenced not only with students but also with teachers. It was confirmed that even teacher educators, when providing professional development, needed to elicit, reframe, or clarify teachers' ideas, press for elaboration, check for interpretation, and connect the content presented with their classroom experiences (Zhang, Lundeberg, McConnell, Koehler, & Eberhardt, 2010).

These types of sustained responses can be encouraged in several ways:

1. If the student's answer is *correct*, ask for further clarification or probe by asking several follow-up questions, which develop answers more fully. *Probing* can provide new insights for students or take what they already know to higher levels.

Some examples of probing questions are:

"What additional information do you need to solve that problem?"
"What would you have to do to get that information?"

USING FUNNEL QUESTIONS TO PROBE

When responding to your questions, students may offer information that is too general or too detailed. You can probe either type of response by funnel questioning. If you are looking for more detail, you can narrow the funnel. This process is similar to that used in deductive reasoning in which the thinking proceeds from general to specific. "Tell me more about . . ." is a general question that guides the responder to give you more information. Since it is an open question, it permits the responder more leeway and gets more detail, even though it may take more time.

Questions that employ words such as "specifically," "actually," or "particularly" will also frequently gain more detail from students.

If a student responds to your question with specific information, you may want to probe him/her by asking questions that elicit information about more general topics. Decreasing the amount of detail is analogous to inductive reasoning in which thinking proceeds from specific to more general.

You can widen the funnel by focusing questions that provide less detail about a small area and increase information about related topics. "What other things," "Who else," "What else" can help obtain this kind of information.

2. If the student says s/he doesn't know the answer or provides a weak or incorrect answer, you can provide *cueing* for that student by offering some follow-up questions that will lead him/her to a correct response.
Example:

Teacher:	What is an adjective?
Student:	I'm not sure.
Teacher:	Last week we played a concept attainment game where you were supposed to learn about adjectives. What were some of the words in our Example column?
Student:	Uh, uh . . . blue, uh, oh yeah, pretty, fat.
Teacher:	Give me a sentence with the word "blue."
Student:	John is wearing a blue shirt.
Teacher:	What does blue tell you about the shirt?
Student:	Tells what it looks like.
Teacher:	What's another word for telling what something looks like?
Student:	Describes.
Teacher:	What word is blue describing?
Student:	Shirt.
Teacher:	What part of speech is shirt?
Student:	A noun.
Teacher:	So what is an adjective?
Student:	Oh yeah, I remember now. A word that describes a noun.
Teacher:	Good thinking.

3. If a student does not respond, you can cue him/her, or say you will get back to him/her, and then use *redirecting* in which you ask the same question (without repeating it) to one or several other students. When the answer or deepened perspective regarding the answer is finally elicited, go back to the original student and have him/her repeat the answer or preferably put it in his/her own words. The point is to have the original student learn and receive satisfaction that s/he has responded correctly. And besides, when the student verbalizes a correct answer, it reinforces and, thereby, helps him/her retain that answer.
Example:

Teacher:	We've been studying mammals for several days. What are some of the characteristics of mammals? (Pause) Henry?

Henry: (No response)

Teacher: Martin?

Martin: They have hair or fur.

Teacher: Excellent. Why would they need hair or fur?

Martin: They're warm-blooded.

Teacher: True. Can anyone think of anything else that makes mammals different? (Pause) Robert?

Robert: They suckle their young.

Teacher: That's right. And one way to remember that is to think of the connection between mammals and mammary glands. Now, Henry (*goes back to first student to whom s/he asked the question*), can you tell us some characteristics of mammals?

Henry: They have hair or fur and mammary glands to feed their babies.

Teacher: Great, Henry. I knew you knew it.

An interesting analysis of a student's incorrect answer was made by Robin Hunter (2004). He pointed out that when a student provides an incorrect answer, there are two things s/he does not know: the correct answer to the question and the question to which the incorrect answer belongs. Hunter offers as an example that when a student is asked how much 5 times 7 is and responds that it is 30, s/he does not know that $5 \times 7 = 35$ and that $5 \times 6 = 30$. As a result, there are two facts the student must learn. He proposes teaching *both* by using the following procedures:

a. Dignify the student's answer by offering the question to which the answer belongs.

   "You would be correct if I asked how much 5 times 6 was because it equals 30. You are already correct to be in the 5 times table." The communication to the student is that s/he had something to offer but just got it in the wrong place.

b. Assist the student by cueing. "If you bought six pieces of gum for a nickel each, how much would that cost you?" (You could draw this on the board and have the student add the number of fives 6 times to get 30.) Then add to the drawing one more piece of gum, and have the student add the extra nickel to the 30 to get 35.

c. Hold the student accountable. The student must learn and remember after being cued. With the drawing still on the board, go back and ask how much 5 times 7 is and then how much 5 times 6 is. Then say, "I know that you will remember this tomorrow." (Adapted from Hunter, 2004, p. 111).

At this point in the review of questioning, it is important to remind you that students from different cultures and students with exceptionalities may view teacher questioning and reactions to responses differently. To ensure equity in dealing with all students, remember the following.

With Asian Americans, where shyness is valued, a student *may* not volunteer and avoid eye contact so that s/he will not be called on.

Students whose native language is not English *may* need a wait-time longer than three to five seconds to respond.

Hispanic females, when in a class with males, *may* be observers during the discussion in the classroom rather than demonstrate academic prowess.

Native Americans *may* be ill at ease when cued or probed.

Teachers *may* ask more questions of boys than girls, direct more questions involving higher levels of thinking to boys, and provide them with longer wait-time.

Learning disabled (LD) students *may* have difficulty answering questions at higher levels. LD students need more time to practice higher-level responses and more time to process questions. It is sometimes helpful for students with learning disabilities to write answers to questions.

Observe that the word "may" was used in all the previous examples to avoid stereotyping. It is difficult and often frustrating for teachers who want to be equitable to deal with the diversity in their classrooms. The best way to handle the diversity in your class is to *explain ahead of time* what you will do and *why* you are doing it. For example, tell the students that you will call on both volunteers and nonvolunteers. Then explain that the reason you will do this is that you want everyone to achieve, and it has been proven that the more they participate, the more they achieve.

INEFFECTIVE QUESTIONING PRACTICES WHEN RESPONDING TO STUDENTS' ANSWERS

In their anxiety to get answers from students, teachers will often engage in behavior that actually impedes the learning process and discourages students from participating. Some of these inappropriate questioning behaviors include the following.

Repeating the Student's Answer (Response)

If you observe classroom questioning, you may be surprised that it is common for teachers to immediately repeat students' answers. This practice seems difficult for teachers to avoid just as the practice of increasing the wait-time after asking a question or repeating or rephrasing questions immediately after asking them. Some teachers may think that they are rewarding students by repeating their answers, reinforcing correct answers, or repeating students' answers so that they can be heard by all class members.

As already mentioned, you should train your students to answer in a tone that everyone can hear so that repeating answers is not necessary. In the contemporary classroom that fosters student support and cooperation, you want to ensure that students do listen to each other. If you emphasize that you value what all students have to say, that it is all right to make a mistake, and conduct your questioning sessions in a nonthreatening way, students will feel more confident speaking up. Besides, repeating students' answers becomes boring, and it subtly signals the rest of the class that they do not have to listen to each other in the first place.

The Tugging Question

When the teacher has elicited enough information but tries to pull (tug) more information, the additional information becomes meaningless.

Example: In a classroom where five attributes of Impressionist paintings are already listed on the board, the teacher says, "Who can give me just one more attribute of these paintings?" The students take a deep breath and then sigh with frustration. Be aware of when you have elicited enough information from students. Then, move on.

Reacting in a Discouraging or Disappointing Manner to Answers You Do Not Expect

As a teacher, you already know to expect the unexpected. Teachers, especially novices, tend to frame questions that have pat answers. As teachers expand their repertoires to include more divergent questions, students may not answer the way teachers have anticipated, causing them to sometimes react in a negative and discouraging way. Borich (2007) provides an example of an inappropriate reaction to unexpected answers. When you read the script, *stop after the first teacher reaction to Student 1*, and think of what response you might expect from the student before reading the rest of the interchange.

Teacher: OK, today we will study the European settlers who came to America and why they came here. Why did they come to America?

Student 1: To farm.

Teacher: No, not to farm.

Student 2: To build houses and churches.

Teacher: No, that's not right either.

(Borich, 2007, p. 326)

How would you feel if you were Student 1 or Student 2? How could you use effective questioning practices already described in this chapter to build on an incorrect answer to get the appropriate student response?

A teacher could ask Student 1 for further clarification by saying, "While farming was of interest to some people, there were more important reasons Europeans wanted to come here. Can you think of any others?"

A teacher could probe Student 2 by asking, "Why would churches be important?" This question would eventually lead to the fact that some Europeans came here for religious liberty.

The teacher should try to accept the students' answers, even if incorrect, in a positive way and try to build on the responses to lead the student to the correct answer.

Paraphrasing a Student's Response in a Way that Actually Corrects an Incorrect Answer Offered by the Student

Example:

Teacher: Why did Europeans come to America?

Student: To farm

Teacher: While some were interested in farming, others came for religious liberty.

Inappropriate Body Language

Several studies (Brophy, 1979; Siegman & Feldstein, 1987) have suggested that nonverbal communication (body language) is perceived as *more powerful* than verbal communication by most students. Frowning, scowling, head shaking, hands on hips, eye rolling, foot tapping, or taking a deep breath and exhaling with a loud puff can discourage students from participating. Also, pointing at a student either by using the whole hand or a finger instead or even calling that student by name when eliciting a response is viewed as accusatory and impersonal. Yet, pointing at students when calling on them is a common practice of many teachers.

ENCOURAGING STUDENT QUESTIONING

In the contemporary classroom that encourages students to write questions for tests, assist in writing criteria for rubrics, and monitor their progress in achieving behavioral and cognitive goals, students should also be encouraged to ask questions about academic content. Yet one of the most neglected teacher questioning skills has been eliciting these types of questions from students (Walsh & Sattes, 2005).

Focusing on student questioning and valuing these questions as opposed to emphasizing responses are critical for teachers who want to move from a teacher-centered to a student-centered classroom (Albergaria-Almeida, 2010). Moreover, it has been reported that students enjoyed reading each other's questions and became more interested in deeper understanding (Drozynski et al., 2010).

When students are first asked to formulate questions, it is an eye-opener for teachers, for the students frequently mirror teachers' behavior. Just as teachers must learn and practice effective questioning skills, so must students. They can be assisted in developing questioning skills in several ways:

General Ways to Encourage Questions from Students

- As indicated in the beginning of this chapter, ensure that you have established a warm and caring classroom environment for your students. This open environment will result in a positive emotional climate that is personal and risk-free. Students who feel personally connected with their teachers and with their classmates ask a higher number of questions (Newman & Schwager, 1993).
- Show that students' questions are valued. Sometimes, students will ask irrelevant questions during a lesson, and the teacher, desiring to stay on task, will tell the students that the question has nothing to do with the lesson. However, if the teacher reserves a space on the board, or displays a poster with a title equivalent to "Questions We Want to Explore" where questions can be recorded during the lesson and pursued later, the teacher can then immediately go back to the lesson, and the students will be rewarded for their questions. It is important, however, that there then be *follow-through* on exploring recorded questions.
- Have the students make a habit of writing questions at the end of a lesson; at the end of a chapter or unit; before and after a field trip, video, or visit by a resource person; and during their reading. Research has shown that when students are required to generate questions about material they have studied or have read, there is a significant improvement in comprehension (King & Rosenshine, 1993).
- Write the lesson objective on the board in the form of a question. When the lesson is completed, go back to that question, have the students answer it, and then ask for additional questions.

  Example: Write the question, "How can we compute the area of a circle?" instead of the objective, "To compute the area of a circle." Ask the students to answer the question, and then ask them if they have any other questions.

- Encourage the formulation and phrasing of students' questions by *modeling* these questions.

For example, when discussing what students have read, ask questions such as:

What is the point the author is trying to make?
What main questions/problems does the author bring up?
What are the author's assumptions?
What evidence does the author present?
How does the author organize the evidence?
What are the author's conclusions?
What makes the conclusions warranted or not warranted?
What is the author's viewpoint?
What implications come from the author's reasoning?
(Bookmark from the Foundation for Critical Thinking, www.criticalthinking.org)

Types of questions that model higher-level thinking in students in any subject could also include:

What is the main point . . .?
How is this related to . . .?
What are the positives and negatives of . . .?
How is . . . different or the same?
What can you conclude from . . .?

In addition, unexpectedly thoughtful discussions were provoked by, "What would happen if . . .?" (Drozynski et al., 2010).

Most important, if the teacher does not know the answer to a question, s/he should display a "let's find out" attitude where the teacher and the students can pursue the answer together and from that answer generate more questions.

- Invite students to question each other using the same positive practices suggested in Phases 1 and 3 described earlier. Reinforce what you should already have established in creating a positive classroom atmosphere— that during the questioning, students must be courteous to each other, not monopolize the discussion, address each other *by name*, and consider each question carefully before framing it.
- Use authentic questions. Students are more motivated to ask further questions when stimulated by *personally relevant* questions and those that rouse their interest in accordance with their age and stage of development.

Table 2.2 presents the best practices criteria for effective questioning.

Table 2.2.   Best Practices for Effective Questioning

During a discussion, recitation, review, or demonstration:
Effective questioning practices in Phase 1: The teacher asks a question to one or more
   students

Criteria (Descriptors)	Performance Indicators (Examples)
set up a supportive environment for student participation	
secured attention of class before asking a question	
asked clear questions	
asked only one question at a time	
phrased questions so that students did most of the talking (higher-level questioning)	
paused at least three to five seconds before calling on a student to respond	
called on students *after* asking the question	
called on students by name	
called on a balance of volunteers and nonvolunteers	
ensured that everyone was asked to participate at least once, *including low-achieving students*	
when appropriate, asked students to write their answers to questions	
demonstrated sensitivity to cultural diversity	

Ineffective questioning practices in Phase 1 (those to be eliminated)
Remember that the criteria described below are negative, and your aim is to have their
   performance indicators remain blank.

Criteria (Descriptors)	Performance Indicators (Examples)
repeated or rephrased questions immediately after asking them	
pointed at students when calling on them	
asked questions requiring yes or no answers	
asked predominantly questions requiring one-word answers	
asked questions requiring a chorus response	
answered own question(s)	
asked leading questions	

Effective questioning practices in Phase 3: The teacher reacts to students' answers

Criteria (Descriptors)	Performance Indicators (Examples)
paused three to five seconds before reacting to a student's answer or asking another question	
gave some feedback to *every* answer	
encouraged sustained responses from all responders, *including low-achieving students*, by appropriate use of asking for further clarification of a student's response, redirecting questions, cueing, probing	
asked a student whose answer was incorrect to repeat the correct answer offered by another student	
asked another student to repeat the question a student called on did not hear	
asked student who did not hear the original question repeated by another student to answer the original question	
encouraged students to ask their own questions	

Ineffective questioning practices in Phase 3 (those to be eliminated)
Remember that the criteria described next are negative, and your aim is to have their performance indicators remain blank.

Criteria (Descriptors)	Performance Indicators (Examples)
repeated a student's answer	
gave no feedback to an answer	
answered or paraphrased correctly a student's incorrect answer when redirecting, cueing, or probing would have been more appropriate	
reacted negatively to a student's answer either verbally or through gestures	
continued to elicit responses on a topic even though enough information had already been obtained	
discussed with colleagues if any changes (modifications, additions, deletions) were needed in any of the aforementioned effective or ineffective questioning criteria as a result of new research	

- Just as you were encouraged to teach students learning theory and how to construct tests, teach students how to question. Questioning is a skill that can be learned, and students should learn the same skills addressed in this chapter. Depending on the maturity of students, teach them the difference between open and closed questions, the need for pausing, and even how to improve their questioning levels according to different taxonomies (cognitive, affective, psychomotor).
- Questioning the textbook. Ask the students to go through different paragraphs in a textbook. For every declarative sentence, have the students write a question that the declarative sentence would answer. Then ask other students to answer the question.
- Take a few moments to share with your students what *you* learned as a result of their responses to questions and to questions they have asked you and the class. This action communicates to students more effectively the value you place on their participations and their questions.

Chapter 3

Increasing Your Instructional Strategy Repertoire

It has been reported that most teachers, even those selected by principals to be mentor teachers—those responsible for developing new teachers—have a limited instructional repertoire, *relying on only one strategy*, thus preventing students from learning (Joyce & Showers, 2002). Acquiring many different instructional strategies is necessary for effective teaching (Marzano, 2003a).

In this chapter, you will learn new strategies to add to your repertoire. Accomplishing this task will provide you the variety that will better match different kinds of objectives with corresponding instruction and help you deal more successfully with the diverse needs of students in your class.

Possessing a strong range of instructional strategies will also give you the flexibility to make your classes more interesting and brain-compatible. Since having a number of different strategies will keep your students more meaningfully engaged in the instructional process, student misbehavior will tend to decrease, thereby minimizing your stress level.

To use a range of strategies successfully, you have to know the theory behind them, how to implement them, and when they would best be applied. This knowledge differentiates professionals from technicians.

There are numerous strategies that can be employed in the classroom (Pagliaro, 2011). Given space limitations, only several can be reviewed. The following sets of instructional strategies go from teacher-directed to student-centered.

CONCEPT ATTAINMENT

Theory Review

A concept is defined as a category that groups similar objects, people, or events. Concepts allow us to put objects into categories and then be able to recognize members of that category (Gagne, Yekovick, & Yekovick, 1993). Dog is a category that includes poodles, terriers, chihuahuas, collies, other pure breeds, as well as mixed breeds. Categories allow us to organize an enormous amount of data into manageable segments. Concepts are the foundation of our thinking and our communicating. We need concepts to learn principles (generalizations, laws, rules) that express the relation between two or more concepts.

It is of prime importance that your students learn concepts well, because once *mis*conceptions occur, they are very difficult to change.

The members of a category or class are grouped together by certain *attributes* or distinguishing features. The attributes may be *critical* or *noncritical*. A chair always has a seat, legs (usually four), and a back support. These are its critical attributes. A chair may also be high, low, wide, or narrow; made of metal, wood, or plastic; and embellished in different ways. These are its noncritical attributes.

All categories do not have clear-cut defining attributes (Benjafield, 1992). Though flying is common to most birds, it is not a critical attribute of its class. If it were, the nonflying penguin or ostrich would not be considered birds. A house is not always a place where people live. It could be the House of Representatives, a house of ill-repute, or a restaurant with a specialty, such as House of Burgers.

Since concepts are abstractions, the only way they can be dealt with is through examples (exemplars), those which belong in the category, and nonexamples (nonexemplars), those which do not belong in the category. However, you recall from the previous paragraph that category membership can be unclear. Schwartz and Reisberg (1991) referred to these unclear categories as those that have *graded membership*. Some objects, events, or people provide better examples of the concept or category than those which have graded membership.

Implementation Review

When applying concept attainment in the classroom, the teacher must first establish the objective s/he wishes to teach (learning the concept in this case) by informing the students that s/he has an idea in his/her mind s/he wants them to guess. The teacher presents several matched pairs that contain examples of the idea, as well as nonexamples. Examples are displayed in the Example column, and nonexamples are displayed in the Nonexample column. The students are to identify the characteristics or attributes of the examples by comparing the examples with each other and contrasting them with the nonexamples. The question the students are to consider is, "What do the examples have that the nonexamples do not have?"

When presenting the set of examples, the teacher should use the *best representatives* of the category known as prototypes (Rosch, 1973). In order to have students concentrate on the critical attributes of the best set of examples (prototypes), it is essential that the prototypes have as *different* as possible noncritical attributes. For instance, in the case of teaching the concept of triangles, the teacher should present triangle examples of different sizes, side lengths, and colors so that the students will concentrate on the critical attribute—a closed figure with three sides.

When presenting the set of example and nonexample pairs, the teacher should make each pair's noncritical attributes as *similar* as possible so that the students can concentrate on the differences between examples and nonexamples. In the case of teaching the concept, two-syllable words, the teacher can use "strangle" as an example and "string" as a nonexample. Since both words start with the same consonant blend, *st*, the students can then examine more efficiently the differences between them.

Look at the following word pairs in Table 3.1 to see how the noncriterial attributes of the examples (words that contain silent letters) are different from each other (in initial letters, number of syllables, parts of speech) and how the example and nonexample pairs are similar.

Example and nonexample sets can be introduced as a single pair first or altogether. Examine the list of examples and nonexamples for teaching the concept, prime numbers (Table 3.2).

Table 3.1. Word Pairs

Examples	Nonexamples
salmon	salad
castle	caddy
Almond	altar
gnat	not
sword	swing
knowledge	kitten
whole	hole

Table 3.2. Prime Numbers

Attributes	Examples	Nonexamples
	7	8
	2	20
	5	4
	11	9

If the teacher introduced just the first pair, 7 and 8, the students might decide (hypothesize) that the attribute "odd number" is possessed by the example and not by the nonexample. The teacher would write "odd number" under the Attributes list even though it is not the correct attribute of prime numbers. At this stage in the lesson, the students' guess would be correct. Since 7 and 8 are both single digit numerals, and, therefore, similar in this respect, the students would not tend to offer "single digit" as an attribute of the example, 7.

In the next matched pair, 2 and 20, the attribute "odd number" would be eliminated, since 2 is even. The students would now have to decide what 7 and 2, both examples, have in common that is still different from 8 and 20, the nonexamples. If the students hypothesize that 7 and 2 are "less than" 8 and 20, the next pair the teacher introduces, 5 and 4, would eliminate the attribute "less than." The students would continue comparing the examples and contrasting them with the nonexamples. The pair, 11 and 9, represents the first time a two-digit numeral is offered as an example, and an odd number, a nonexample. This pair may further assist in the comparing and contrasting. Eventually the students should come up with the fact that the numbers represented by the examples have only themselves and one as factors. They have guessed the teacher's idea—that some numbers are only divisible by themselves and 1 (attribute of the concept). The students can then be told that these numbers are called prime numbers (the label).

If a student offered the actual concept, prime numbers, as an attribute, the teacher would have to ask for the attribute(s) of prime numbers. *If the student cannot identify its attributes, s/he does not know the concept.* Eventually, the students can be told that 1 is a special number that is a factor of all numbers. It is a special number called the unit that is neither prime nor composite.

Many suggestions by the students might be unanticipated, and the teacher, even if s/he plans the matched pairs carefully, must be armed with or think "on the spot" of additional examples and nonexample pairs, which eliminate noncritical attributes to finally elicit the critical attributes of any concept s/he wishes to teach.

The same examples offered above can be presented all at the same time instead of one by one. The students would then compare all the examples and contrast them with the nonexamples to come up with the attribute(s). The teacher may still need to offer additional example and nonexample pairs.

Once the essential attributes of a concept are identified, the students basically know the concept. This is true whether or not they have a label (name) for the concept. *The name or label is less important than knowing the attributes.* However, eventually the set of attributes has to be labeled.

Remember that knowing the label is not necessarily the same as knowing the concept. Students will often use labels for concepts without having a clear idea of their attributes. A typical example is a kindergarten student who may verbally state the name "six" but cannot count six objects if they are positioned differently. The same student may also count the same object more than once or skip the object.

Adults often use terms they do not fully understand. Most adults thought that the term "impeach" meant that a president could be thrown out of office instead of that the president would undergo a trial to see if s/he should be removed.

When a student uses a term and you are not sure whether or not s/he really understands it, *ask for an example*. Also ask for a nonexample because in understanding a concept, a student should know what it is, as well as what it is not.

The teacher further determines whether or not the students know the concept by offering one at a time in random order different examples and nonexamples, which the students have to place under the correct column. Students must state *why* they have made their placement choice. The next step is having the students offer their own examples and nonexamples and also list them in the proper columns. At this time, the students should be able to explain or justify why their offerings are examples or not. In the final step, the teacher has the student apply the concept to deepen understanding. Students may identify prime numbers in their textbooks, anywhere else in the environment, or use prime numbers to do prime factorization.

It is more effective to present nonexamples that do not all belong to the same category. This was unavoidable in the prime number example where all the nonexamples had to be composite numbers, those that had other factors besides themselves and 1. However, if "adjective" is the concept to be taught, the teacher should display nonexamples that represent various other parts of speech such as verbs, adverbs, conjunctions, pronouns, adverbs, prepositions, or interjections. Using nonexamples from different categories makes it easier to contrast the examples and nonexamples so that the critical attributes of the examples stand out.

Examples and nonexamples can take many different forms (Table 3.3). They can be sentences.

Table 3.3. Examples and Nonexamples as Sentences

Examples	Nonexamples
Walking is good for you.	You are *walking* too fast.
I like *walking*.	*Walking* away from the accident, Tom shook his head.
With *walking*, you get good exercise.	While he was *walking*, he tripped on a rock.

Underlining the word "walking" allows the student to concentrate on the use of that particular word in sentences. Given enough examples and nonexamples, the student should be able to recognize that in the examples, walking is the -ing form of a verb that is used as a noun, not as a participle (assuming the student knows before the lesson what a participle is). The concept the teacher has in mind is gerund.

Examples and nonexamples can be symbols or pictures. If the attributes of Impressionist paintings were to be identified, all the examples would be paintings from that period, and the nonexamples would be paintings from *several other* periods.

A concept attainment lesson can also be taught using an expository or direct presentation form instead of an inductive approach. Using the expository method, the teacher would begin by identifying and defining the concept. Then s/he would provide the critical attributes of the concept and identify examples and nonexamples. In the final step, s/he would have the students offer their own examples and nonexamples. Even though the expository approach can be effective, the inductive approach presented earlier, where the students must discover the attributes for themselves, gets the students more actively involved mentally, and discovery is a better memory technique. Table 3.4 presents the best practices criteria for concept attainment.

Table 3.4. Best Practices for Concept Attainment

Criteria (Descriptors)	Performance Indicators (Examples)
The teacher determined whether students were experientially ready for the new concept	
informed students that s/he had an idea (concept) they were to guess	
informed students that examples and nonexamples of the concept would be presented and the students were to identify the attributes (distinguishing features) of the concept by comparing examples and contrasting the examples with nonexamples	
presented and displayed an initial positive example (prototype), which clearly contained *all* the essential attributes of the concept and wrote this example under the Example column	
presented immediately afterward an initial nonexample, which contained *none* of the essential attributes of the concept and wrote this nonexample under the Nonexample column	
requested students to contrast the example with the nonexample and state what attributes the example had that the nonexample did not have	

Criteria (Descriptors)	Performance Indicators (Examples)

listed the elicited attributes under the Attributes
   heading

presented an additional example and nonexample

asked the students to compare the examples and
   contrast them with the nonexamples

eliminated attributes from the list, which were not
   possessed by all the examples

provided more example and nonexample pairs
   and had students compare the examples and
   contrast them with nonexamples until all essential
   attributes of the examples were identified and
   nonessential attributes were eliminated

provided in all examples noncritical attributes of the
   examples that were very *different*

provided in all example and nonexample pairs,
   noncritical attributes that were very *similar*

asked the students to examine the examples
   to determine if the identified attributes were
   possessed by all of the examples

If a student offered a category (concept) as an answer
   instead of attributes,

asked the student to clarify what the category meant
   (give its attributes)

presented one-by-one a random mixture of examples
   and nonexamples and asked students to place
   them in the proper column

asked students to explain *why* they put the examples
   and nonexamples in the selected column

requested that students create their own examples
   and nonexamples and place them in the proper
   column

asked students to explain why the suggestions they
   offered were examples or nonexamples

provided experiences for students to apply the
   concept

CONCEPT FORMATION

In the concept attainment model just presented, students were asked to determine the attributes of a concept the teacher wanted them to learn. The students then compared examples of the concept and contrasted them with nonexamples. In the concept formation model, students must make a decision regarding how they will develop (form) categories from attributes.

Theory Review

The concept formation model was developed by Taba (1967) in a social studies curriculum where lessons, units, and entire courses integrated thinking with content. Taba developed her strategy upon certain assumptions.

- The student can be taught to think. The teacher should assist the student in developing inductive thinking.
- Thinking results when there is a transaction between the student and data. The teacher guides students in this transaction by presenting them with data from different sources, having them organize the data, connect items in the data, and then make generalizations and inferences.
- Thought processes come about in a "lawful" sequence. Skills build on already mastered skills. It is the teacher's role to ensure that prior skills are achieved before continuing with other skills (Joyce & Weil, 2000).

Four different inductive thinking skills have been developed from Taba's model—concept formation, data interpretation, application of principles, and conflict resolution—along with corresponding teaching strategies for each one. In this section, only the first, concept formation, will be discussed.

As already indicated earlier in this chapter, the development or formation of concepts is the most basic form of knowledge. Concepts are building blocks without which other cognitive processes cannot take place. Principles and generalizations depend on the relationships between or among concepts, and problem solving depends on principles and generalizations.

Implementation Review

Concept formation has three parts: *data collection*—securing and enumerating data relevant to a topic being studied; *data grouping*—reorganizing the data into categories with members having the same attributes; and *group labeling*—giving a name to the categories developed. The result, according to the theory, should be the formation of major concepts from broad categories of related data.

In the first part, collecting the data, the data may be listed by the students or given by the teacher. For example, if you were asked to list the data in this chapter so far, you might include the following: system, teacher-directed strategy, concept, model, attribute, example, concept attainment, prototype, category, strategy, nonexample, graded membership, group, or matched pairs of examples and nonexamples. These data could also be provided to you by your instructor. Listing data is an important skill because it involves differentiating relevant from irrelevant information. Every student can participate in this process, regardless of ability.

In the second part, grouping the data, students classify the data and justify the classification. In the preceding example, students might group prototype and example together because they should both be the best representatives of a group, or they should be examples dissimilar enough so that the students can focus on critical attributes. Students might group example, nonexample, and matched pairs of examples and nonexamples together because they help find attributes. Strategy, system, and model may be grouped because they generally mean the same.

The teacher guides the students in grouping the data through clear directions:

- Focus the grouping on the basis of common attributes, *not* labels.
- Create at least five or six groups. If this number is not specified, students, especially with their first experience with concept formation, may be apt to form one similar group and classify the rest as "other."
- Include all of the data in the grouping. No items should be left out.
- An item of data may be used in more than one group.

After all grouping is completed, the groups are displayed on the board or on posters. In this way, students share their groups with one another and can readily see that a member of one group can also hold membership in another or others. From the original data, students may also suggest additional data items to place in groups formed by peers. Students of all abilities can participate at their own levels with lower achievers more apt to form groups with more concrete or descriptive items and higher achievers likely to form more abstract groups.

During the third part of the concept formation strategy, labeling the groups, the students must assign a phrase or word that describes what is the same about all the items in the group. "Things that are made of metal," "Things that are made of metal and wood," and "Breakfast foods" are examples. After all the groups are displayed and labeled, the teacher fosters the discovery of new attributes and different relationships among the items and labels. For example, students can see that an item of data can fit into several different groups. Eventually the students are encouraged to discover hierarchies in the relationships by determining which labels can include others and which can fit under other labels.

Concept formation is an excellent activity to employ at the end of a unit, a chapter, or after reading a story to conduct review, discover new relationships, or deepen understanding. Table 3.6 summarizes the best practices criteria for concept formation.

Table 3.5. Best Practices for Concept Formation

Criteria (Descriptors)	Performance Indicators (Examples)
Data Gathering	
After studying a unit, topic, chapter, or novel or taking a field trip and the like, the teacher asked students to enumerate relevant data or provided corresponding data for students	
If the data were provided by the students, the teacher ensured everyone's participation in the data gathering	
ensured that all students understood each item of data	
elicited data *without* concept labeling	
Data Grouping	
instructed clearly how to group data	
asked students to explain their grouping	
provided a means for displaying all groups	
Labeling	
asked students to identify a label for the group	
asked students to check that each item in the group fit the label	
asked students to check the items in the group for additional attributes	
asked students to check for other items in the data that may belong in the group	
asked students to make associations between and among labels	
identified hierarchies among labels	

THE ADVANCE ORGANIZER

Theory Review

David Ausubel (1963) was an educational psychologist concerned with meaningful as opposed to rote learning. To understand his theory, consider the following paragraph adapted from Davis (1983):

Pteropus is a member of the Pteropidae family of Megachiroptera.
Unlike members of Microchiroptera, Pteropus eats fruit . . . roosts in trees, looks like a fox, and uses its eyes quite a bit. (p. 219)

Do you think you know what Pteropus is? Probably not. Most teachers do not know when they read the paragraph. The important consideration is *why* they do not know. Do you think you know why?

The reason is that there is nothing in the paragraph to associate Pteropus with what the reader already knows. If the paragraph began stating that chiroptera is the scientific label for bats, the reader would likely have the cognitive structure (category), bats, to associate with Pteropus.

Ausubel's theory is relatively simple. "If I had to reduce all of educational psychology to just one principle, I would say this: The most important single factor influencing learning is what the learner already knows. Ascertain this and teach him accordingly" (Ausubel, Novak, & Hanesian, 1978, p. iv). Connecting new material to ideas or categories previously learned gives *meaning* to the new material. This principle was subsequently verified by neuroscientists (Jensen, 1998).

The existence of a set of categories, a cognitive structure, is the main factor that determines learning. Learning occurs when new material is included or "subsumed" into an existing cognitive structure by hooking new concepts to old ones. The teacher should be familiar with general inclusive concepts of the discipline s/he is teaching. These general inclusive concepts known as *subsumers* provide what Ausubel calls anchorage with which to incorporate new material. The most general inclusive concepts are introduced to the students all at once, in advance. The inclusive concepts should be reviewed with the students after which more specific content can be introduced. The concepts are structured in a downward hierarchy from general to specific, with the broadest categories on top and the more differentiated concepts underneath (Joyce, Weil, & Calhoun, 2004).

Ausubel (1997) has identified the broad inclusive concepts as advance organizers. The purpose of the advance organizer is to close the gap between what the learner already knows and what s/he needs to know before s/he can successfully learn new material. Advance organizers are familiar concepts the teacher uses to hook or anchor new information. Since the organizers go from top to bottom, they provide explaining power with which to absorb new material. In the paragraph presented at the beginning of this section, knowing the category "bat," the advance organizer, can make it easier for a student to understand the different sizes, mega and micro, as well as distinguishing characteristics of bats of each size. Using meaningful broad concepts on which to hook new information makes the new learning more efficient, thus reducing the chances of forgetting.

Implementation Review

To accomplish the previously discussed theory, there must be top-down communication with a process of progressive differentiation. In this process, the most inclusive and general ideas are presented first. Then more detailed and specific ideas are progressively introduced. Finally, there is a process of integrative reconciliation, where new ideas are carefully related to (integrated with) prior learning.

There are two types of organizers: expository and comparative. The expository organizers are larger organizers (concepts), which include the new material, thus allowing anchorage for more detailed new material. Doctor is an expository organizer that includes physicians, PhDs, dentists, chiropractors, podiatrists, veterinarians, or anyone else with the title, Doctor. Comparative organizers are at the same level as that of new content. They allow the student to compare and contrast similarities and differences among concepts at that level. Physicians, dentists, PhDs, chiropractors, and optometrists are comparative organizers with different functions, training, and expectations, and, therefore, these doctors are able to be distinguished from one another.

The advance organizer is useful when it is introduced at the beginning of a unit, a chapter, a topic, or a novel, particularly when there is a lot of *verbal material* to be learned. Once the students absorb the mind-set of the general content organization, they learn where new information fits into that organization.

The advance organizer is not the same as a semantic web or graphic organizer, which may be arranged in an order *other than* a hierarchy. The advance organizer is always presented in a hierarchy. Even though the organizer is deductive as opposed to inductive in nature, it still engages students by having them establish relationships between and among concepts, thus keeping students meaningfully involved in learning.

Figure 3.1 presents an example of an advance organizer.

Table 3.6 presents the best practices criteria for the advance organizer.

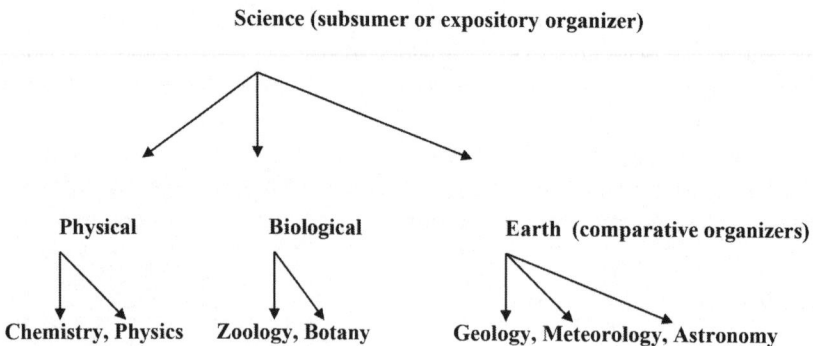

Figure 3.1.   An advance organizer

Table 3.6. Best Practices for the Advance Organizer

Criteria (Descriptors)	Performance Indicators (Examples)
Planning	
The teacher identified the major organizing concepts of the subject for him/herself	
arranged subsumers in a hierarchy with the "largest" (most inclusive) on top	
identified attributes of each subsumer	
identified examples of each subsumer	
identified comparative organizers	
placed subsumer (expository) organizers on a higher level than comparative organizers	
placed comparative organizers on the same level	
Presentation	
The teacher presented to students in writing the entire advance organizer	
emphasized connections between the new material and what the students already knew	
presented attributes of each subsumer	
presented examples of each subsumer	
compared similarities and dissimilarities between and among the subsumers	
asked students to put in their own words the attributes of the subsumers	
asked students to compare and contrast the attributes of the subsumers	
asked students to explain the relationships in the advance organizer	
kept the advance organizer displayed	

MODELING

Theory Review

Initial research regarding the effects of learning through models has been conducted by Miller and Dollard (1941), Bandura and Walters (1963), and Bandura (1969, 1974). A foremost authority on the subject of modeling, Albert Bandura, has demonstrated that exposure to models can produce four separate results: the *observational learning (modeling) effect*; the *inhibitory effect*; the *disinhibitory effect*; and the *response facilitation (eliciting) effect*.

Observational learning (modeling) allows a person to acquire an entirely new set of behaviors (response repertoire), by observing the performance of others. Think of how you learned how to hold eating utensils, pronounce words, develop speech patterns, respond to disappointment, or react to getting a cut on your finger. Chances are you learned how to behave through observing models, in most cases your parents or caretakers or peers.

Through the inhibitory effect, inhibition or suppression of previously learned responses became strengthened. Observers who saw models punished for misbehavior tended to decrease their own similar misbehavior.

Through the disinhibitory effect, the inhibition or suppression of previously learned behaviors became weakened. Observers who saw models rewarded for misbehavior tended to increase their own similar misbehavior.

In the response facilitation (eliciting) effect, the behavior of the model influenced the observer by facilitating a response repertoire (set of behaviors) already present in the observer. The model provided discriminative cues that triggered similar responses in the observer.

Most of the research regarding modeling was focused on deviant behavior. When applied to the teacher in the classroom, the application of modeling concentrated on developing observational learning, and this type of learning will be the thrust of this section.

Teaching new behaviors through observational learning, modeling, has always been used in schools. Students have learned how to swing a bat, bend glass, cut a pattern, or pronounce a word in French through modeling. More recently, modeling has been used by teachers to demonstrate thinking skills, such as analyzing out loud the thought process involved in solving a math problem, or demonstrate affective skills such as dealing with students with learning or physical disabilities. Bandura (1986) and Schunk (1987) have added new research to verify that modeling is an efficient way to acquire new behavior, especially when reinforcement and practice are key components. It has also been demonstrated that even peer models can be effective in teaching skills to classmates (Schunk, 2000; Schunk & Hanson, 1985).

Implementation Review

To teach through modeling, attention must be directed toward the desired behavior. These may be behaviors involving procedures (lining up for lunch or dismissal), skills (threading a sewing machine), or mental processes (problem solving). It should be perfectly clear in the teacher's mind what steps are necessary to reach the desired behavior. The teacher should be able to explain and demonstrate the task. Throughout the demonstration, the students' attention should be focused on the task. The students should then be allowed to rehearse the task with constant feedback, both positive (reinforcing) and corrective. Best practices criteria for modeling are listed on Table 3.7.

Table 3.7. Best Practices for Modeling

Criteria (Descriptors)	Performance Indicators (Examples)
Preparation	
The teacher identified the task to be achieved	
analyzed the component parts of the task by breaking it into segments (steps) and subsegments (substeps), when necessary	
prepared a list of clear labels for the segments and subsegments	
prepared cards identifying each label	
Implementation	
clarified the task for the students	
checked to see if the students could restate the task (in their own words)	
listed the steps necessary to completing the task	
listed the substeps involved within each step, if the task called for it	
demonstrated how to perform the task	
While performing, explained each step along the way	
placed the corresponding label card next to each step	
identified substeps	
placed the corresponding label card next to each substep	
After performing, asked the students to identify the steps	
identify the substeps	
use the correct term (label) to identify each	
Student Practice	
The teacher allowed each student to practice the task	
provided positive feedback for each step implemented correctly	
provided corrective feedback for steps implemented incorrectly	
During the practice, asked the students to verbalize each step and substep	
asked students give positive and corrective feedback to each other	
allowed enough practice time for mastery	

The Lecture Background Review

The lecture has been used for centuries. It transmits information by "covering" a lot of material, and the *assumption* is that what is said in the lecture is internalized by the listener. The lecture uses telling as a medium, thus providing one-way communication in which students learn through one sense only—hearing. Listening to a lecture is an abstract way of learning and is, therefore, the least engaging.

Research has demonstrated that the average student's attention span during a lecture is from 10 to 20 minutes, considerably less for younger students (Penner, 1984; Ryan, Cooper, & Tauer, 2008), and that attention is cyclical (Ericksen, 1978). The student's attention (therefore, possibility for retention) is highest at the beginning of a 40- to 50-minute class, subsides considerably after the beginning, and then increases to some degree just before the end. This cycle is present even with a dynamic lecturer, though it was demonstrated that when actors delivered lectures as opposed to instructors, students achieved more (McLeskey & Waldron, 2004).

Think about the following:

Lectures have bad reputations. Maybe you're familiar with

the sayings, "telling is not teaching" and "the sage on the stage."

Chinese proverbs tell us that "What I hear, I forget" and popular

wall charts read "I remember 5% of what I hear, 10% of what I

see." All of these sayings condemn us to using any modality

other than telling. This is nonsense. It depends on *what* you tell

and *how* [italics in original] you tell it. (Hunter, 2004, p. 46)

The lecture integrates several different theories. You have already read some of them in earlier sections of this chapter. If a lecture is to be used, there are several ways to make it more effective for students.

- Make sure that you know the material very well.
- Begin the lecture with a hook that involves the students. When you studied how to write a composition, you were told to make your first sentence an attention-getter to capture the readers' interest. Do the same with listeners.
- Organize the material so that it can be presented in approximately 10-minute segments. This organization will make the next segment new again and take advantage of the 10-minute attention span of most students.
- Summarize important points at the end of each segment, or better, ask the students to summarize them. "The critical element of a lecture is to diagnose the amount of information students can process before they must interact with it" (Hunter, 2004, p. 47).
- Use visuals. They help clarify verbal content and assist students who are not auditory learners (Cruickshank, Bainer Jenkins, & Metcalf, 2003).

- Provide vivid examples. When you read the concept attainment strategy earlier in chapter 2, you noted how important clear examples were to learning concepts. Take advantage of using these clear examples to enhance students' understanding and involvement.
- Use advance organizers (presented earlier in this chapter). These organizers put the content you present into perspective and assist the students in making associations with the content.
- Ask questions intermittently. Questions keep the students engaged and will give both you and them a means to determine how well content is being assimilated.
- Avoid reading your lecture. Prepare in advance key ideas you want to present, order of presentation, and important definitions and examples, and then write them on 5 × 8 cards so that they are more readily visible. Before the lecture, rehearse what you want to say. Rehearsing what you want to present out loud will help you clarify your own thinking. Avoiding reading your material verbatim will also allow you to use a more conversational tone in your delivery, keep eye contact with your students, and constantly monitor their reaction.
- Vary your presentation to avoid passive listening and attention loss (Wolvin, 1983). You can vary the stimuli by changing the pace, moving around the room, telling relevant but brief anecdotes, and using body language to convey important ideas and heighten emotional involvement.
- Remember that in a lecture, less is usually more. It is better that you cover less material that the students learn than a lot of material that does not get processed.
- Deliver your lecture with enthusiasm. It is contagious.

Table 3.8 presents the best practices criteria for implementing lectures.

Table 3.8.   Best Practices for Delivering Lectures

Criteria (Descriptors)	*Performance Indicators (Examples)*
The teacher prepared thoroughly the lecture content	
introduced the lecture with a hook that engaged the students	
organized appropriate amount of material that could be processed (approximately 10-minute segments)	
requested that the students summarize major points at the end of each segment	
incorporated visuals	
offered vivid examples	
provided advance organizers	
asked questions intermittently	
varied the presentation	
delivered material without (major) reading time	
presented material with enthusiasm	

PROBLEM-BASED LEARNING

Theory Review

The seeds for problem-based learning (also known as project-based learning) were sown by some of the theorists with whom you are likely already familiar as well as from education courses such as Foundations of Education and Educational Psychology.

The philosophical thrust to problem-based learning has been presented by Dewey (1916), Thelen (1960), and Michaelis (1963). They all believed in the idea that the school should be a miniature social system that reflects what citizens need to do to maintain a democratic society. In this mini social system, students face the same types of problems that citizens must solve, those that draw from all fields and utilize academic inquiry skills.

These methods are supported by cognitive and social psychologists. Piaget (1952) proposed that children must be actively involved in their own learning. Through this interaction, children construct representations regarding their experiences. With continued experiences, these representations in time become more sophisticated and abstract. Bruner (1961) determined that the most important learning comes through personal discovery that occurs through active involvement in learning. Vygotsky (1978) added the dimension of sociocultural aspects in learning. He believed that to understand human activity, the context in which it takes place must be examined. It is in the social interaction that occurs within the culture that cognitive structures and thinking processes are created and developed. Social interactions with peers as well as with adults provide a means for "bouncing off" ideas that advance the student's cognitive development.

Teachers, often frustrated with the passive learning prevalent in schools, began looking for alternative ways of teaching other than by transmitting information through lectures, discussion, rote learning, and "covering" a wide curriculum by teaching subjects in isolation. They wanted an approach that would use higher thinking skills where students were involved in self-directed inquiry in decisions that affected their lives and where intrinsic motivation would drive the learning process. Brain research has verified that elaborate rehearsal and "hands-on" activities are necessary for most learning and that studying a subject in isolation does not readily allow for the transfer of learning (Jensen, 1998). Teachers have found that an alternative method that fosters elaborate rehearsal, higher cognitive thinking, a deepening of understanding, and thematic instruction is problem-based learning.

Implementation Review

The underlying idea in problem-based learning is that the goal of education is not to have students do well in school but to have them do well outside of school. Therefore, students are presented with a real problem, an authentic problem that is meaningful to them. The problem should be challenging—one that adults wrestle with in the real world. If the problem is not authentic, does not actually affect the students personally and/or socially, it should at least be engaging. The best problems are current. The problem may be one offered by the teacher or one suggested by the students. There may be a single solution to the problem or varied solutions, but the solution(s) must be genuine. The problem takes an extended time to complete, usually several weeks.

Once the problem is defined, it becomes the focus of instruction. Goals follow from the problem. Students learn different problem-solving skills. These may be the scientific method, or a modified version, depending on the nature of the problem. You may remember that the scientific method has several important steps.

- The problem is specified and students must understand all the terms in the problem before they can go on.
- Tentative guesses (hypotheses) are offered to solve the problem.
- Each hypothesis is individually tested by gathering data.
- Each hypothesis is retested to check results.
- On the basis of hypothesis testing results, one or several hypotheses are selected to solve the problem.
- The solution is then implemented.
- The solution is monitored to see if it is producing the desired results.
- If not, the above process is repeated until the problem is solved.

In order to test each hypothesis, data must be collected from several different subject areas, allowing students the opportunity to integrate knowledge from different disciplines. The students engage in a collaborative effort to collect and analyze data and select solutions. Collaboration itself is an important out-of-school mental activity with the problem providing a context for thinking (Resnick, 1987). Working together is also more motivational and develops social skills. Students may work in pairs or in another small group arrangement. As they work together, they share ideas, discuss solutions, and use real concrete objects such as computers, calculators, or scales. The nature of the activities allows the students to construct their own meaning regarding real-world phenomena. The *process* in which they are engaged is as important as the solution.

When a solution is offered by a group, they must go beyond communicating this solution in the traditional forms such as reports, dioramas, or collages. Students must produce authentic products to demonstrate what they have learned and how the problem was solved. Exhibits, videos, models, mock-ups, pamphlets, brochures, and computer programs are some examples of products the students can create. The products are then shared with the other groups who may have come up with different solutions.

The teacher's role is most critical in determining the success of problem-based instruction. S/he serves as a coach and a model for the problem-solving skills his/her students will need (Stepien, Johnson, & Checkley, 1997). S/he must ensure that students believe that they can solve the problem, have enough competence to do so, and can relate their success to *effort*. Attitudinal and verbal communication of the teacher is encouraging and keeps the students' attention on the process involved in solving the problem as well as in developing the end product.

Of equal importance is setting up a structure in the classroom that will ensure success. This structure necessitates that the teacher provides access to materials to assist the students in the investigation, monitors the interaction between or among students, and encourages students to think for themselves and express their points of view. The teacher must be able to manage logistical and organizational problems in order to ensure that work flows smoothly. Where will materials be stored? How can the environment where many different groups are working on different tasks be controlled? What types of arrangements must be made for out-of-class research the students must conduct in the school library or with resource people or places within the community itself? If one or several groups finish early, what should be done to keep them involved until the other groups complete their work?

It must be pointed out that though there are many positive characteristics of problem-based learning, there are also several concerns. Given the organizational school structures and prevalent time for meeting learning standards, problem-based learning is a difficult strategy to implement. The strategy needs the support of library and technological resources, which can be expensive. Only a limited amount of information can be covered using this approach. Grading of students' work is a persistent issue. And finally, the teacher must have the knowledge to be able to draw from many different disciplines and the managerial skills to keep the students on target. Table 3.9 offers the best practices criteria for problem-based learning.

Table 3.9. Best Practices for Problem-Based Learning (T)

Criteria (Descriptors)	Performance Indicators (Examples)
The teacher presented students with a developmentally appropriate authentic problem or presented a developmentally appropriate authentic problem suggested by the students	
ensured that the problem was solvable in more than one way	
presented a problem capable of being solved through drawing on several disciplines	
explained the scientific method for problem solving	

Criteria (Descriptors)	Performance Indicators (Examples)
provided practice in the scientific method for problem solving	
assisted each student in determining what contribution s/he would make in helping solve the problem	
provided adequate resources and materials for solving the problem	
explained how the resources and materials could be used	
established a system for storing materials	
assisted students in selecting partners or small groups	
encouraged students to discuss and explore aspects of the problem	
encouraged students to express their ideas about solving the problem	
kept students focused on work	
assisted students in determining suitable final products	
allowed students to share and present their final products	

MASTERY LEARNING

Theory Review

Mastery learning is a type of individualized instruction which assumes that almost all students are capable of mastery (high achievement) given sufficient time and the correct instruction. Its roots are in behavior theory with its focus on specific learning objectives, small units of instruction presented at a time, and immediate feedback and rewards for accomplishment. Benjamin Bloom (1968, 1976) is the major proponent of mastery learning. Bloom's work, based on prior work by Carroll (1963), has demonstrated that mastery learning permits approximately 80 percent of students to attain a level of achievement ordinarily reached by only 20 percent using other methods. The challenge persists regarding what to do with the remaining students who do not achieve mastery.

Mastery learning employs certain *assumptions* and implies a specific instructional model. It assumes that

- quality learning is possible for most, if not all students;
- for quality learning to take place, the *instruction* must change;
- some students may need more time than others;
- most learning follows sequential and logical steps;

- most learning outcomes can be expressed in observable and measurable terms; and
- students can be successful at each level of instruction, thus providing them with the incentive to advance further.

Implementation Review

In the mastery learning strategy, the instruction is individualized. The teacher ensures that certain features are present in the instructional design. The student's knowledge is preassessed to pinpoint areas of weakness. This preassessment is often referred to as a diagnostic test or pretest. The teacher discusses the results of the pretest with the student, and together they decide what goals and objectives would be desirable to improve performance. The objectives are stated in specific, behavioral terms.

A signed contract is set up between student and teacher agreeing how the objectives will be implemented, how often the teacher will check work, and how long it should take the student to complete the contract. Older students will be able to spend more sequential time working on the contract than younger students. Input regarding how the student likes to learn is also received at this point, and the teacher makes every effort to include the student's suggestions as part of the instructional component.

A personalized packet is designed for the student. This packet, also referred to as a learning activity package (LAP) or a self-instructional package (SIP), contains the objectives or small set of objectives, specific practice activities the student performs to achieve the objectives, and an assessment to inform the student how well s/he is meeting the objectives.

The activities are structured and expressed clearly enough so that the student can implement them without the teacher's presence, leaving the teacher free to work with other groups or individual students. To make sure that the contract is personalized, directions and instructions should be written in a conversational tone. "You will be able to add fractions with unlike denominators" is more personal than "The student will be able to . . ." For students who cannot read yet, the instructions can be prepared on tape.

The instructional activities should be engaging, varied, and attractive and include auditory, visual, and tactile/kinesthetic modalities. These could include computers, manipulatives, videos, magazines/newspapers, models, and diagrams. If after working on the practice activities the objectives have still not been met, corrective instruction is provided (instruction is recycled) until the objectives have been attained. It should be obvious that if a student does not achieve the objective using one instructional activity, a *different* instructional activity must be made available. The student is then allowed to continue to work on the remaining sets of objectives with immediate feedback and more recycling, if necessary. After the student has completed all of the objectives, s/he takes a posttest to determine how well she has mastered the material. In many cases, the pretest and posttest are the same, and there should be an appreciable difference in achievement demonstrated in the posttest. If not, a new contract is established with different instructional strategies.

SIPs do not necessarily have to be designed for remediation. They can also be used as enrichment for students who need challenge or as makeup work for students who missed class due to absence or visits to the psychologist, speech therapist, instrumental music teacher, or any other member of the school staff.

Mastery learning is particularly effective when the student needs to develop concepts or skills that serve as a foundation for additional learning. Best practices criteria for mastery learning are listed on Table 3.10.

Table 3.10. Best Practices for Mastery Learning (T)

Criteria (Descriptors)	Performance Indicators (Examples)
The teacher administered a diagnostic test (pretest)*	
established goals and objectives of instruction (preferably with the student, when age appropriate) on the basis of pretest results	
prepared a packet with a set of sequenced objectives grouped in small segments	
secured ideas for activities from the student's suggestions	
prepared varieties of activities to meet the objectives (integrated different learning modalities)	
prepared packet using unique formats and designs to make it more attractive to the student	
wrote directions and instructional activities using the pronoun "you"	
prepared an assessment for each objective (though one assessment may cover several objectives)	
determined with the student a realistic daily schedule and time frame for completion	
If a contract evolved, signed the contract and had student sign the contract	
determined a reward for successful completion of contract	
administered a posttest to determine achievement	
If the posttest did not demonstrate growth, prepared an alternative activity for each unachieved objective	
filed packet for future use for a student with similar needs (no need to reinvent the wheel)	

* When using the packet for enrichment or for makeup work, the diagnostic test would not need to be administered.

LEARNING ACTIVITY CENTERS (LEARNING STATIONS)

Learning Activity Centers (LACs) are miniature versions of the open class-room. In the open classroom, the curriculum is not set or delivered by the teacher in a formal sense, but rather by developmentally appropriate materials placed in the classroom. Students decide the materials with which they would like to engage. The role of the teacher is to keep track of what the student is doing and intercede to ensure that learning is occurring as a result of the engagement. On the basis of what the students are achieving, the materials are changed so that students can continue interacting with new materials and grow and learn from that process.

Theory Review

The open classroom received its main impetus from the Progressive move-ment spurred by the work of John Dewey (1916) and was further promoted as an instructional method by educators due to the developmental theory of Piaget (1954).

Dewey saw education as a process that provided experience and action rather than a focus on purely academic work. He saw education as holistic, where the whole student, his/her interests and abilities, had to be taken into account before planning any curriculum and instruction. An environment had to be set up where students had to actively participate in their own learning. The curriculum had to be child-centered where the child learned by doing.

Piaget believed that humans inherit the ability for organization and adapta-tion. During the organization process, students make sense of their world by gathering and arranging their information into psychological structures. With continued experience, these structures are further combined and coordinated to form more sophisticated structures (schemas), which help us "think about" the objects and events that occur in the environment.

Humans also have the inherent ability to adapt to their environment. They do this through assimilation and accommodation. In assimilation, humans use their existing psychological structures when they come in contact with new information or experience that fits with what they already know. In accom-modation, humans must adjust their existing psychological structures to respond to new information or a new situation. Assimilation and accommoda-tion are constantly used as people face increasingly complex environments.

The open classroom responds to the interactive, experiential environments supported by Dewey and Piaget. However, when open classrooms were implemented in the 1920s and 1930s and rediscovered in the 1970s, they were not successful in providing needed knowledge and skills. Many schools that were built with open designs gradually had those designs replaced by walls that separated classes in the same way as they were in more traditional education.

Implementation Review

The LAC provides a modification that can be used to reap the positive effects of the open classroom while maintaining for the rest of the class more structured approaches. Also known as a learning station, the LAC is a sectioned-off location within the classroom. There may be more than one station in the room. Students usually work at the center individually, though they may work in pairs. The center can be used for enrichment, reinforcing information after a lesson, making up work, interacting with new content when a task is completed, or for remediation. The teacher provides all materials students need in order to work at the center. Since the center is self-contained in this respect, the student can work alone without the teacher's presence, though the center is often supervised by a paraprofessional.

Unless the center is designed for an exploratory activity where the students can work with materials to see if there is anything unique they can come up with, the center needs structure. This structure is often presented in the form of a chart, poster, activity cards, or audio/videotape, which gives instructions regarding how the materials are to be used. Dewey (1938) warned educators that there was a difference between an activity and an experience. His warning was again addressed by Hutchings and Wurtzdorff (1988). Dewey noted that students can be working with materials, being involved with an activity indefinitely. But it is the teacher's role to make sure the activity is turned into an experience, which Dewey defined as making a connection with the activity and the learning that the activity should produce.

For example, a student can be playing with tongue depressors (pipe cleaners, toothpicks) placing them one on top of the other and making different types of designs for a long time, and that has some value. But the teacher should ensure that the student can count 10 tongue depressors, put a rubber band around them, leaving him/her with one group of tens. S/he can then slide the tongue depressors out of the rubber band to get back his/her 10 groups of one. If the teacher did not provide this structure, the student might play with the tongue depressors without ever realizing that one group of 10 is the same as 10 ones.

This regrouping is an essential prerequisite to addition and subtraction of two-digit numerals. Thus, the activity, playing with the tongue depressors, was turned into an experience, learning that one group of 10 (one 10) and 10 groups of one (10 ones) are two different names for the same number, 10. Therefore,

Table 3.11. Best Practices for Organizing Learning Activity Centers (LACs)

Criteria (Descriptors)	Performance Indicators (Examples)
The teacher decided the purpose for setting up the LAC	
(specific cognitive knowledge, discovery, exploration, enrichment, review, skill development, etc.)	
related the topic of the LAC to the current curriculum	
determined the specific objectives of the LAC	
informed the students of the purpose of the LAC	
prepared an attractive LAC	
selected materials that integrated several disciplines, whenever possible	
provided a variety of materials appropriate for achieving the objectives	
provided safe materials	
posted clear instructions and activities for using materials (or taped instructions for nonreaders)	
arranged for the LAC to be supervised by an aide/ volunteer	

the instructions provided by the teacher in the center ensure that the learning objective(s) the teacher has in mind for having the students engaged with the materials at the center are achieved. Table 3.11 presents the best practices criteria for establishing a learning activity center. Table 3.12 summarizes when to use specific instructional strategies.

STRATEGY SUMMARY

Table 3.12. A Summary of Instructional Strategies

Strategy	When to Use
Concept Attainment	To ensure that students can identify critical attributes of a category (concept). This knowledge is a prerequisite for learning principles, generalizations, and solving problems
Concept Formation	To deepen understanding/discover relationships at the end of a unit, chapter, story, novel
Advance Organizer	At the beginning of a unit, novel, chapter, topic when a lot of verbal material is to be learned
Modeling	To teach new skills (physical, thinking, or affective)
Lecture	To "cover" a lot of content

Strategy	When to Use
Problem-Based Learning	To solve appropriate authentic problems suited to the developmental level of students
Mastery Learning	To provide tailor-made individualized instruction that is self-correcting
Learning Activity Center	To offer individual students new material, enrichment, reinforcement, makeup work, remediation, or a free-time assignment

Chapter 4

Managing Your Classroom More Productively

REVIEW AND UPDATE

Classroom management is a comprehensive process that integrates all inter-dependent components—student knowledge, an engaging curriculum, robust instruction, developing students as responsible learners, and self-reflecting teachers (Hanson, 1998). The most crucial component of classroom management is setting up an environment that makes instruction flow smoothly with minimal interruptions and student misbehaviors.

Starr (2003) stated that Harry Wong, an educational expert, has indicated that classroom management involves routines and procedures that foster the teacher's ability to teach and the students' ability to learn. He claims that teachers who can teach, manage their classrooms. These teachers are educators. Teachers who can't teach, manage their students. These teachers are bullies.

Not only is skill in managing a classroom a major factor in determining the success of a teacher (Brophy & Evertson, 1976), but in reviewing over 11,000 subsequent research studies, skill in classroom management was found to be *the* most important factor with respect to its effect on student achievement (Evertson & Weinstein, 2006; Wang et al., 1993).

Though you may believe that teaching academic subject matter should be your top priority, the reality is, "You will never be able to conduct instruction and effectively teach your class until you are able to manage the behavior of *all* [italics in original] of your students" (Canter, 2006, p. 123) with the goal of having them eventually manage themselves. Canter goes on to say that you will actually save academic teaching time as well as energy by putting management first.

Curriculum and instruction also have to reflect the needs of the twenty-first century. This means that students must be involved meaningfully in learning, because if they are not, they will find their own ways to become engaged, often to the detriment of themselves and to the rest of the class.

Students should be invited to add their own curriculum goals in addition to those of the teacher; be given choices regarding how they will learn; self-reflect and monitor their goal achievement; redirect their effort, when necessary; and play an essential role in their own assessment/evaluation.

Students should be involved in relevant experiences and authentic problems and, when age appropriate, should participate in constructing scoring rubrics. Depending on the situation, students may work independently or in groups, check each other's work, and coach when warranted, with all individual members taking responsibility for the group's achievements and supporting each other to attain success.

In short, designing/implementing the curriculum and classroom management have a symbiotic relationship. Each depends on the other for support, and each enhances or detracts from this relationship.

Parenting styles have changed within the past thirty years from a tendency to be more rigid and authoritarian with a do-as-I-say-because-I-said-so approach to a more nurturing, permissive, do-as-you-want approach to bringing up children. Research has indicated, however, that neither of these approaches used by parents, or teachers for that matter, will prepare children for the twenty-first century (Marzano, 2003a; Steinberg, 1996).

What is most effective is an *authoritative* (not authoritarian) approach which "balances nurturing with setting clear limits, giving guidance without controlling, seeks input from children for important decisions, sets high standards of responsibility, and encourages independence, not dependency" (Cummings, 2000, p. 9).

As classrooms in the twenty-first century become more student-centered, both teachers and students must adjust accordingly. Classrooms are now becoming learning communities in which there is *shared responsibility* for the success of all community members. Within this context, there has been a shift in emphasis from teacher control to the student's taking more responsibility not only for his/her own learning but also for managing the classroom.

While in the past teachers were taught to control student behavior, now teachers are focusing on developing strategies that support students' making good choices (McLeod, Fisher, & Hoover, 2003). Teachers and students listen carefully to each other. Feedback is prompt on the part of both. There is a sharing of leadership between teachers and students as the teacher no longer controls but fosters student self-control and responsibility.

The teacher determines rules collaboratively with students who participate in determining both rewards for following and consequences for not following rules. There is shared responsibility for implementing and enforcing rules. This sharing is particularly important because "a sense of efficacy, control, or self-determination is critical if people are to feel intrinsically motivated. When people come to believe that the events and outcomes in their lives are mostly uncontrollable, they have developed learned helplessness" (Woolfolk, 2008, p. 371).

The classroom atmosphere is warm, friendly, and caring. All class members have mutual respect for and support each other in a spirit of cooperation in which all have a stake in the success of all other members. It is the purpose of this chapter to assist you in using these principles to improve your skills toward being a shared leader in classroom management.

CLASSROOM MANAGEMENT AND STUDENT MISBEHAVIOR

When thinking of classroom management, problems with student misbehavior frequently come first to mind. Misbehavior problems are often associated with discipline or punishment, though discipline and punishment are *distinctly different*. Discipline is guiding the student's personal, social, and cognitive development in a way that will minimize misbehavior, thus making punishment, the imposition of a penalty, unnecessary.

Make no mistake about it. *All teachers have classroom behavior problems.* It is the main complaint about their job (Kottler, Zehm, & Kottler, 2005). Some teachers have fewer discipline problems than others, and if you implement the guidelines presented in this chapter, your problems should be minimal.

PROACTIVE APPROACHES TO CLASSROOM MANAGEMENT

Just as in medicine it is better for the patient and more cost-effective to prevent disease, so is classroom problem prevention better for both you and your students. It has been reported that 90 percent of classroom management occurs *before* students misbehave (Franklin, 2006).

In a study that has become an educational classic, Kounin (1970) compared problem-free classrooms with those that were disruptive. His research found that teachers in both types of classrooms usually handled disruptive problems similarly *once they arose*, but the teachers who had few problems were those who used certain preventive techniques. Kounin identified these as withitness, group focus, overlapping, and movement management.

Withitness. A teacher who has withitness is aware of everything going on in the classroom whether s/he is looking directly at the students or not. The teacher's antennae are pointed in all directions. S/he interacts with everyone, not with just a few who are allowed to monopolize attention. Eye contact is maintained with all students, making them realize that the teacher is noticing their behavior. A withit teacher knows who the real troublemakers are, intervenes quickly before disruption gets out of control, and when two or more problems are brewing, handles the more (most) serious one first.

Whereas the traditional teacher might be satisfied being just withit, a contemporary classroom manager goes beyond. S/he seeks feedback from students to determine *why* they may not be meaningfully engaged. This teacher constantly asks him/herself why some students may remain on the brink of or be actually involved in misbehavior, analyzes the problem with the class, and proceeds to correct the problem with class recommendations, whenever appropriate.

Group focus. A teacher who demonstrates group focus keeps all students involved during instruction. If one student is misbehaving, the teacher communicates expectations through the "ripple effect," correcting that misbehavior to alert students in the rest of the group considering or exhibiting the same misbehavior to correct theirs.

As the teacher moves about the room to check the work of different groups, s/he employs current techniques to keep everyone on target. Students may temporarily conduct or continue with a lesson. A group of students may write answers to questions and check each other's answers. The teacher constantly circulates about the room to keep in physical contact with everyone.

Kounin's emphasis on the importance of having the teacher moving around the room has been supported by the research of Hall (1977), Scollon (1985), and Bowers and Flinders (1991). Student involvement varies directly with distance from the teacher. The closer the distance between teacher and student, the greater is student involvement and communication, with less opportunity for the student to become disruptive.

The contemporary classroom manager, while involved with group focus, wants to know *why* the students may be misbehaving. This teacher asks the students for their input and assesses the situation accordingly. As shared leaders in classroom management, students are responsible for implementing and enforcing classroom rules. The *students* alert misbehaving students regarding their responsibilities to themselves and to the rest of the class.

Overlapping. The teacher with overlapping skills keeps on top of several different activities at the same time. S/he may check one student's math, spelling, or lab report while keeping an eye on a small group or work with one group that is writing a play while supervising two other groups who have different assignments regarding that play. If a student from a group other than one the teacher is working with raises a hand, the teacher uses a gesture to acknowledge the student without interrupting the group with whom the teacher is working.

The teacher makes sure that students within each group have assigned responsibilities, not only to each member of the group but to all other class members as well. Students have input regarding what these responsibilities should be and how to implement them. They are agreed to collaboratively, clarified, and practiced so that all students know what to do regarding their assignment, how each member will contribute to that assignment, and how to handle any problems that may occur.

Movement management. The teacher who can manage movement keeps the class active at an appropriate pace. S/he has a sense of timing, knowing when to speed up, or change the activity. There is an absence of slowdowns where the lesson comes to a standstill or when students do not have anything to do when they have finished their work.

Slowdowns also occur through *overdwelling* commonly referred to as "beating a dead horse," where the teacher keeps teaching content (or rules) long after the students have mastered them. Transitions from one activity to another are smooth, and there is an avoidance of *flip-flops* where the teacher begins an activity and then reverts back to the prior one; *dangles* where the teacher begins an activity and then stops and leaves it hanging; or *fragmentation* where the teacher breaks up a learning activity into *very* small segments.

It should be mentioned that even though Kounin's work was introduced in the 1970s, his suggestions are still supported (Emmer et al., 2003a, and Emmer et al., 2003b).

The contemporary classroom focuses more on group work, especially after an initial lesson has been introduced. In the spirit of involving students in classroom management, the contemporary teacher asks the students for their suggestions regarding what activities might be offered when completing work ahead of time, what signals they might give the teacher when they feel that they "got it" so that overdwelling is not necessary, and when and how instruction can be changed to be more effective, thereby avoiding flip-flops, dangles, and fragmentation.

When extending Kounin's preventive techniques to contemporary classroom management, the teacher and students should remind misbehaving students when their behavior is not supporting other class members and interferes with the learning of others. As such, this misbehavior will not foster the cooperation that will lead to the success of every student in the class, which is an integral attribute for the twenty-first-century classroom.

CREATING A POSITIVE CLASSROOM ATMOSPHERE

Besides the preventive measures described by Kounin (1970), there are other proactive techniques teachers can use to establish a successful learning community. The most important of these is creating positive student–teacher and student–student relationships in a classroom where all feel welcome and are responsible for making other class members welcome.

The teacher might say something like this to the class: "We are in this together. When one of us succeeds, we all succeed. When one of us fails, we all fail. It is critically important to me personally that all of us do well." This is a very powerful message. Of course, *the teacher must implement the implications of this message consistently.*

To emphasize the aforementioned point, Brooks (2011) has described the successful classroom as engaging and well managed. In this classroom, there is a strong interrelationship between student and teacher in an atmosphere of trust in which students feel free to participate. Brooks promotes the idea that there is a partnership between classroom management and student learning. Both thrive when trusting, respectful, caring relationships exist between students and teachers. Only then will rules become effective and students become engaged learners.

In constructing this positive classroom climate, three main factors should be considered. They involve the students, the teacher, and the learning environment itself.

THE STUDENTS

It has been a criticism of teachers and administrators that they do not ask the right questions when it comes to classroom management (Kohn, 2003). He suggests that instead of asking how we can get students to obey, we should ask what our students need and how we, as educators, can meet those needs. Because we are focused on getting students to conform, we fall back on practices of doing things *to* them as opposed to working *with* them. This section will concentrate on working *with* students.

Fundamental to contemporary classroom management is fostering caring relationships and finding positive characteristics of students (Rigsbee, 2008). There are many different ways to accomplish these.

Kohn (1996) makes the point that students do not become more likely to think for themselves or care about others when teachers take all responsibility for rules and expectations for student behavior and consequences for noncompliance. He encourages teachers to assist students in becoming compassionate, in assuming responsibility, and in reflecting by taking the unpredictable and likely messy route. This involves having the students work together in deciding how to be fair and in determining what respect means.

Traditional approaches to classroom management would likely have teachers informing students what rules would be expected to be followed. Twenty-first-century managers, however, show students that they are respected, valued, and trusted by giving them a stake in the successful operation of the classroom.

Successful contemporary managers *have students participate in establishing rules and procedures* (Curwin & Mendler, 1999; Marzano, 2003b, 2007) *and do so at the very beginning of school.* A rule conveys a general expectation that can be applied in many different circumstances, such as "Listen when others are speaking"; a procedure states a course of action for a routine such as a method for passing out or collecting materials. Rules/procedures should be reasonable, clear, short, *explained,* practiced when applicable, displayed, and minimal with approximately five to eight for elementary school students (Emmer et al., 2003) and around seven for middle/secondary school students (Emmer et al., 2003).

There is a difference between behavior and classroom management. Behavior is related to discipline, and classroom management has to do with procedures and routines.

According to Wong and Wong (2005), teachers who are ineffective discipline students with consequences and punishments whereby teachers who are effective manage their classrooms with procedures, rules, and routines. Please reread and think about the previous sentence.

Taking time to explain rules and procedures is highly recommended because in order to be implemented, they must be understood (Good & Brophy, 2003). It is also effective to explain the reasons *why* the rules are important. This practice is especially important for students whose cultures may not be compatible with rules and procedures normally implemented in American classrooms.

Rules should be *reasonable.* There are four criteria for reasonable rules and procedures. They must be necessary, capable of being performed by the students, not run against human nature, and not require for their enforcement more resources than you can afford (McLeod et al., 2003). When establishing rules, the teacher should concentrate not only on what to do with students who do not comply with the rules but even more important on what these students are being asked to do as well (Kohn, 1996).

Effective classroom managers are aware of the importance of making instruction more personal by getting to know their students by name right away and immediately *calling them by name.* Contemporary classroom managers make it a point to learn something personal about each student and use this information in instruction. When students are involved personally, they become more involved emotionally. And "emotions . . . are not the cards at the game table but the table itself" (Jensen, 2005, p. 80).

Learning students' names and positive information about them quickly may be more difficult in departmentalized classes, prevalent in middle/high schools where teachers can be assigned 125 students or more. Still, make a concerted effort to know each student, *and the sooner the better*. Plan an activity to have all your students get to know each other by name, also, and address each other by name during class.

Some teachers distribute 5 × 8 cards to all age-appropriate students and ask them to write a symbol or word that best describes them. Then, each student in turn states his/her name and what the rest of the students should know about him/her and explains what the symbol or word communicates.

Whenever the occasion allows, offer students the opportunity to talk about themselves. "People like to talk about themselves and the things that interest them" (Marzano, 2007, p. 114). Providing this activity allows students to remain emotionally involved in learning, especially when you connect what you know about them personally and/or their interests to the knowledge and skills to be studied.

As a contemporary manager who is aware of feedback provided by students, show that you are aware of and sensitive to students' feelings. Try to pick up on attitudes that may come across in art work, written work, or during discussions. *You teach students how to treat you and each other by the way you treat them.* If you show respect for and are courteous and sensitive to all students, they will tend to model your behavior back toward you and toward each other.

In the culturally diverse twenty-first-century classroom, be genuinely curious about different cultures represented by your students. However, always remember that each individual is different and may not conform to the cultural norm. Social scientists will confirm that there are greater differences between individuals *within* a group than there are *between* groups. The prior sentence is so important that you should repeat it to yourself in *different* words.

Ask students to share their customs with you and capitalize on these customs during instruction. Also, try to demonstrate that you have *heard* and understand students' feelings by paraphrasing some of their comments made in frustration or anger.

Paraphrasing by teachers was promoted by Gordon (1974) and is still effective today. If a student says, "I hate chemistry," you, as a sensitive, supportive teacher, could paraphrase by saying, "You're having difficulty balancing this equation" (paraphrase). Then you could add, "Let's see if we can work together to balance it."

Make sure that all students are active participants in *meaningful* activities. Prepare a sociogram for each class. Identify who are the *isolates*, the students selected by no one or very few classmates as those with whom they would like to work, and the *stars*, the students picked by many classmates as those with whom they would like to work.

Attempt to pair or group the isolates into instructional activities with more socially accepted students so that all will feel welcome in the class. Isolates will be more welcomed by socially accepted students if, at the beginning of school, you have established and then continuously reinforced a supportive classroom environment.

In recent school shootings, one common factor regarding the perpetrators was that they were loners. Some reasons for feeling that they were loners could be explained by a popular song that conveys the message that you are only somebody when somebody loves you and cares about you. In a successful learning community, everyone should feel as though s/he is *somebody* and that all class members, especially the teacher, are bonded with and care about him/her. Bonding is especially critical for middle and high school students.

> Being liked by teachers can offset the effects of peer rejection in middle school. And, students who have few friends, but are not rejected—simply ignored by other students—can remain well-adjusted academically and socially when they are liked and supported by teachers. (Woolfolk, 2008, p. 453)

Formerly, there was an emphasis on what students could *not* do. As a twenty-first-century classroom manager, go out of your way to identify the strengths of each student. Let students use their strengths and interests in helping you set goals, modes of instruction, and assessment. When a student accomplishes a task, be sure to encourage him/her.

A productive way to encourage is by sending "You" messages. Consider the difference between the two columns in Table 4.1.

In the past, teachers were advised to use "I" messages, statements regarding what the teacher thinks or feels. The control was in the hands of the teacher. In a student-centric classroom, "You" messages emphasize the positives that *students* have performed not what you feel about what they've done.

Table 4.1.   Comparing "You" and "I" Messages

"You" Messages	"I" Messages (General)
You did a great job helping Larry learn his multiplication facts.	I think you did a great job helping Larry with multiplication.
You worked so hard on your composition that you raised your score 10 points.	I'm proud that you raised your score 10 points.
You cleaned up so well after lab that the other students imitated you.	I liked the way you cleaned up your lab table.

In the "You" messages, the student is in control. Students should feel positive about what *they* have achieved and what control they have taken in applying their own effort.

THE TEACHER

Positive teacher behavior is an effective problem preventer. There are several positive teacher behaviors worth noting.

If there was ever an occupation requiring a sense of humor, it is teaching. If you have one, you possess many advantages. Interacting positively with students is easier, teaching is less stressful, and students enjoy your classes more. In addition to having a sense of humor, you should also be willing to laugh, *even at yourself*, when unanticipated humorous events occur in the classroom.

As a shared leader, never lose sight of the fact that you are a role model, a *critical* role model for your students. Behave as a mature person they can look up to by using proper speech, grammar, and by dressing professionally. While clothes may not make a person, they can be major factors in *un*making a person (Wong & Wong, 1998).

Research reveals that the clothing worn by teachers affects the work, attitude, and discipline of students. You dress for four main effects:

1. Respect
2. Credibility
3. Acceptance
4. Authority (Wong & Wong, 1998, p. 55).

Teachers often complain that they do not get the respect awarded by other professions. Their colleagues retort that those teachers may not be well groomed, may even speak and behave like the students, making it difficult for *all* teachers to gain public and student respect.

When using language in the classroom, some dos and don'ts were recommended by Ryan et al. (2008) and are listed in Table 4.2.

Table 4.2. Professional Classroom Speech

Dos	Don'ts
Speak clearly and concisely	Use filler words such as "uh," "like," "you know"
Use gender-neutral terms	Address students as "Guys," "You guys," or "Fellows." Say instead, "Class" or "Boys and Girls"
Use proper grammar	Use expletives or profanity

(Adapted from Ryan et al., 2008, p. 75)

Shared learning partners admit to making a mistake or not knowing an answer to a question. This behavior on your part shows that you are a person who takes responsibility, thus providing a good example for your students. They will also respect you more for your admission. Convey the message that it is all right to make mistakes. We all do, and what is most significant about mistakes is that we learn from them and try to do better; mistakes help us grow. And if we do not know the answer to a question, what is even more important is that we learn how to find the answer.

Establish a positive but realistic level of expectation not only for academics but also for behavior. When working with the students to establish rules and procedures, convey the attitude that you know your students can learn subject matter and behave properly, and *do not give up on any student*. The confidence you exhibit will often give students the extra incentive they may need.

Many successful people can trace their success, or possibly their redirection in life, to the fact that one person, usually a teacher, believed in them and encouraged them, especially with the support of the class. *You* have the potential to be that person.

As a contemporary classroom manager, be responsive to students' reactions and feedback by constantly assessing and changing immediately, with the suggestions of the students, whatever instruction or method of dealing with improper behavior is not working. Model flexibility by trying out new teaching strategies, new materials, or new activities. If you are not particularly creative or innovative, you can still be resourceful.

At this point it would be useful to note that it is a myth for teachers to think that all misbehavior problems can be prevented, even if dynamic materials and activities are used to keep students' interest (Long & Frye, 1985). Some students are subject to mood swings and peer and home problems, which could affect the classroom even when the teacher offers exciting experiences.

In a successful learning community, a teacher wants to promote a cooperative spirit through shared leadership and developing student self-control. Show that you are aware of the fact that "control over one's life is something that everyone wants and needs. When we don't get it, we go after control over others. Because many of our discipline problems in school either start or end with a power struggle, it is a good idea to look at the idea of sharing control with the students" (McLeod et al., 2003, p. 66).

One small caveat regarding self-control should be pointed out. In some cases, self-control could be inhibitory, especially in the situation when the self-control does not make sense. When exercising self-control, it is more important to have the ability to choose whether and/or when to control oneself rather than merely comply in every situation (Kohn, 2008).

An example would be exhibiting self-control in not pushing another student. However, if an object was about to fall upon that student, it would be beneficial to push him/her out of the way.

Offer students structured choices. Doing so communicates to students that they are competent, in control within limits, and responsible for their own behavior (Fay & Funk, 1995). Besides, choice helps students practice decision making, allows opportunities for students to showcase themselves, and helps students learn that school is relevant to their lives. For teachers, choice is the best way to differentiate (Tedrow, 2008).

Choices can be offered for behavior as well as for instruction. The choices should be authentic and mutually acceptable. There is no point in asking a student if s/he prefers to miss gym or complete an assignment, if going to gym is his/her favorite activity.

Interact with your students in a friendly (not overfriendly) but business-like manner. "A businesslike classroom refers to a learning environment in which the students and the teacher conduct themselves in ways suggesting that achieving specified learning goals takes priority over other concerns" (Cangelosi, 2008, p. 58). Remember that you do not have to be loved by your students; you have to be respected. Students do not like or respect teachers who let them get away with misbehavior.

"The foundation of student respect is based on the premise that you and the class care enough about each other to make sure they behave in a manner that is in their best interest and the best interest of others" (Canter, 2006, p. 26). But you should also note that students like teachers who are trusting and caring and who treat students with respect. When students believe that teachers care for and value them, the students are more cooperative in complying with teachers' requests. These teachers have more influence on students than teachers not so perceived (Jones & Jones, 2003).

Caring teachers→→→ Student appreciation→→→ Student cooperation

  Be fair but firm. Keep your promises and avoid reprimanding or punishing the entire class when only a few are responsible for misbehavior. When some students are misbehaving, have the class first discuss the misbehavior and then determine what should be done about it before you intervene.

Part of being fair is being aware of the halo effect, "the tendency to view particular aspects of students based on a general impression, either positive or negative" (Woolfolk, 2008, p. 618). For example, when a student is particularly cooperative or friendly, a teacher may assign a higher grade based on those attributes instead of on what the student actually achieved or assuming that a student who is a member of a particular ethnic group will be a behavior problem.

Do not necessarily accept other teachers' evaluations of students. Students behave differently with different teachers, and it may be what the teacher does that causes students to behave in certain (undesirable or desirable) ways. It is also essential to remember that in today's diverse classroom settings, fair no longer means treating everyone the same but "trying to make sure each student gets what s/he needs in order to grow and succeed" (Tomlinson, 2001, p. 23).

THE LEARNING ENVIRONMENT

Contemporary classroom managers ensure that they establish a positive classroom learning environment. There are several ways to establish this type of environment.

Provide physical and emotional safety. Ensure that all students feel safe, both physically and emotionally (Jensen, 1998). The classroom must be a place where students feel they can take risks, ask questions, answer questions, make mistakes, admit they do not know an answer, or come up with a "wacky" idea without verbal or nonverbal ridicule from anyone in the class (Tomlinson, 2001).

Part of this safety involves the physical set up of the classroom. It should reflect the activities that are part of your curriculum. These could include areas for large group and small group activities, storage space, a teacher desk location with a favorable vantage point, a library, work stations, computer placements, and a quiet space.

However, critically important are the physical safety considerations in setting up your classroom. Among these are keeping aisles wide and clear, seating students away from doors, connecting and routing electrical cords to prevent tripping, and keeping dangerous objects/materials out of the reach of students.

It would be an effective practice to draw a plan of your room, determine what is movable and what is fixed, and allocate space accordingly at the beginning of the school year. But as the class progresses, it would also be effective to seek student input regarding how the classroom arrangement could be improved. For an in-depth discussion of setting up the physical layout of the classroom, see Pagliaro (2012).

Show enthusiasm. Create a learning environment in which your enthusiasm is picked up by the students. It is likely that you have been in classrooms where the teacher did not seem to want to be there, and/or even appeared bored, which made it more difficult for you to feel excited.

Make every student feel important by arranging some work the student can display or present.

Videotape students working on meaningful projects or students not working productively. Show the video and have the students provide input regarding how *their* work habits were successful or how productivity/behavior can be improved. Take pictures of students who are meaningfully and actively involved, and display their pictures on the bulletin board with an appropriate title such as, "We Are Great" or "We're Almost There." Hard work gives students a feeling of accomplishment.

Always have enough for the students to do. Free or unstructured time is conducive to off-task behavior. Typically, these times occur when students enter the room, when the teacher takes the roll, or when students finish their work ahead of time.

Sponge activities are *substantive* learning activities, which absorb free time and can be recommended by or negotiated with students. Sponge activities may include reading a book, working on a computer program, completing a project at the LAC, or completing a warm-up assignment that is written on the board so that students have something to work on when they enter the classroom (Boynton & Boynton, 2005).

Provide opportunities for all to succeed. Set up an environment in which you teach for success, and there is a pervasive expectation of progress. Evaluate work and assignments to ensure that students are not involved in busy work but are being challenged at their cognitive levels.

When appropriate, give students choices of goals, methods of implementation, and methods of assessment. Use scoring rubrics as teaching tools to assist students in self-improving. When age appropriate, involve students in constructing scoring rubrics. Provide the appropriate amount of stress. Not enough stress offers students little or no challenge, and too much stress turns them off (Jensen, 1998).

Give students a break occasionally. It boosts morale to skip an assignment or a quiz or to do something of one's choice for a period instead of the designated activity for that period. Get the students' input with respect to breaks they might enjoy.

Connect and interconnect. Make a sincere attempt to bond with all students, and ensure that all students feel bonded with each other. Show that you are interested in your students as people.

Try to have a personal chat with each student to find out more about him/her and what together you can do to make him/her successful. "When teachers consciously had personal conversations with students for more than two minutes at a time over 10 days . . . they saw an 85% improvement in classroom management for that student" (Franklin, 2006, p. 5). He uses the analogy of a cramped muscle in dealing with students, especially the most behavior-challenged. Students desire a positive personal connection with an adult authority figure, and when they get that positive connection, the muscle relaxes over time leaving the students free to concentrate on learning (Franklin, 2006).

Acknowledge the personal/positive. Occasionally *recognize* something personal or positive in each student. Statements such as, "You wear a lot of bright shirts," or, "You've shown great improvement in your computation skills," go a long way in keeping you and your students connected. When a student behaves in a positive manner or accomplishes a challenging task for his/her performance level, it would be worth your while to recognize these achievements by communicating with the home through calling, sending an e-mail, a note, or a certificate of good behavior/accomplishment (Marzano, 2007).

Create a learning environment that is safe from bullies. Bullying in schools has become a scourge in this country. Researchers have concluded that students who bully other students rarely do this alone and that bystanders are involved in 85 percent of bullying incidents (Viadero, 2010). It has been reported that "bullies, their victims, bystanders, parents, teachers, and other adults in the building are all part of an ecology in schools that can either sustain or suppress bullying behaviors" (Viadero, 2010, p. 1)

Fifteen percent of the school population has suffered extreme anxieties from bullies, with 75–90 percent having experienced some kind of harassment (Hoover & Oliver, 1996). In a study conducted at the University of Florida (2008), it was reported that in particular, social bullying in adolescence, such as gossiping or spreading rumors, has been linked with anxiety and depression in the victims during early adulthood.

It is also important for you be alert to potential bullies. Contrary to the perception that bullies are the most popular students or most socially outcast, research conducted over a several-year period found that students in the middle of the school social hierarchies are more likely to be bullies (Shah, 2011). Early detection is particularly critical because several studies have indicated that bullying on the part of young children may be early signs of violent tendencies, delinquency, and criminality (Orloff, 2008).

Even though they have problems in and out of school, bullies are not always disliked. Many achieve high social status (Rodkin, Farmer, Pearl, & VanAcker, 2000). Some bullies are quite popular, particularly among their early adolescent classmates who see them as "cool" (Juvonen, Graham, & Schuster, 2003).

Bullies can attack their victims physically, verbally, or online. Cyberbullying has become so rampant in schools that states have begun to enact antibullying laws (Engel & Sandstrom, 2010). Bullies will frequently manifest their behavior by shunning tactics that include not letting a student sit at a lunch table or ignoring certain classmates during sports events (Haber, 2007).

It has been reported by West (2009) that a study conducted over 2005/2006 by the National Institutes of Health noted the following trends:

> Verbal bullying (making fun of victims, teasing in a mean way, calling victims mean names, saying something nasty about a person's race or religion) was the most prevalent form of bulling;
> Boys are more likely to be involved in both physical (hitting, punching, pushing, shoving, kicking, and locking a victim somewhere in the school) and verbal bullying;
> Girls are more likely to ostracize their classmates or spread rumors;
> Most bullying occurs in middle school, particularly in seventh and eighth grades, and declines thereafter;
> Black adolescents, compared with whites, were more likely to be bullies, and correspondingly less likely to be victims;
> Hispanics, compared with whites, were more involved in physical bullying but were more likely to suffer cyber bullying.

The study also noted that the number of friends a student has was significant in determining hostile behavior. Students with many friends are at higher risk of becoming bullies; students with fewer friends are more often victims of bullies.

Engel and Sandstrom (2010) have concluded from their research that our students lack a sense of responsibility for each other's welfare. To address this void, they recommend that schools "teach children how to be good to one another, how to cooperate, how to defend someone who is being picked on and how to stand up for what is right" (p. A2).

If you employ the guidelines in this chapter to establish positive student relationships, these guidelines should address the aforementioned issues and will also work with bullies. Communicate to them positive expectations, show off their successes, and provide public and private recognition (Boynton & Boynton, 2005).

In particular, bullies generally have potential for leadership. However, the bully's leadership is distinguished from that of other students in his/her lack of empathy (Haber, 2007). The teacher should channel the potential leadership ability of the bully in a constructive direction by providing opportunities for management roles in the classroom such as leading discussions, tutoring other students, and assuming classroom responsibilities (Beane, 1999).

Videotape your class periodically. It would be interesting for you and your students to observe how they interact with you and how they interact with each other. Spend some time first analyzing the tape yourself and then having the students analyze it so that you can elicit their reactions and recommendations for improvements.

In conclusion, Michael Anderson, a math teacher who had a disastrous first year, and eventually became his district's Teacher of the Year, finally came up with his recipe for a successful classroom. "Earn students' respect, create an environment where it's safe for them to try and even fail, and then make the material relevant to their lives" (Gammill, 2010).

ELIMINATING TEACHER-CAUSED STUDENT MISBEHAVIOR PROBLEMS

Some negative teacher behaviors that do not belong in a successful learning community include:

Sarcasm and ridicule. You may recall being in a classroom where the teacher or other students made sarcastic remarks directed at you. Teachers who indulge in sarcasm, ridicule, or humiliation invite vindictive behavior from students, especially from students in middle or high school.

Example: A teacher once said to one of his 10th-grade students, "You should see a witch doctor," and the student retorted, "When are your office hours?"

Some teachers may also try to get students to behave properly or do academic work using inappropriate remarks and/or name-calling such as, "When will you wake up?" "We've done this already; what's wrong with you?" or "Don't you get it yet, Dumbo?"

Carrying a grudge. If you have a negative encounter with a student, let the student know that *it is over* so that s/he can begin again.

Example: Jim "removed" some pens from the teacher's desk. The next time pens were missing, the teacher accused Jim of taking them, though he was innocent.

How do you think this accusation on the part of the teacher might affect Jim's future behavior? If the teacher, instead, would have asked the entire class if anyone had "borrowed" the pens, this request would have shown Jim that he was not being charged unnecessarily.

Also, reaching out to a student with a note, phone call, or e-mail after a negative incident will go far in avoiding further unpleasant experiences (Canter & Canter, 2001).

Example: Mr. Wills sent this e-mail to his 12th-grade student.

Hi Hector,

We had a disagreement today, but now it's over. Let's start again.

Be sure to shake my hand when you come to class tomorrow. I look forward to it.

Mr. Wills

You can see how the tone of this message is conducive to a new beginning with the student.

Favoritism. Part of being human is that we have certain preferences. It is normal to like some students better than others. But few things turn off students more than teachers who show these preferences by having pets. In a twenty-first-century learning environment in which all members support each other, this behavior on the part of teachers is unacceptable.

Be aware of some behaviors that show preferences. Teachers who call on and praise the same students, smile at them exclusively, and make them stars of class plays or monitors while ignoring other students cause resentment. Remember that cooperation is your goal. You can likely identify from your past some teachers who favored certain students. Consider how these teachers demonstrated favoritism and how that behavior affected all students in the class.

Making a Case Out of the Most Minor Infraction, Especially in the Presence of Others

Example: Jenna is chewing gum. The teacher says, "Jenna, are you a baby who constantly needs something in your mouth? You'd be better off sucking your thumb." The class laughs.

Another version of making a case out of chewing gum occurs when the teacher addresses this "poem" to gum-chewing Jenna.

A gum-chewing girl,
And a cud-chewing cow,
What is the difference?
I know now,
The intelligent look on the face of the cow.

The entire matter might have been handled by a traditional teacher saying to Jenna, "Put the gum in the waste basket." However, a contemporary classroom manager would first ask Jenna herself (and if there is no response, the class) if she had violated a rule, and if so, what *she* should do about it. Remember also that an effective twenty-first-century teacher would have made sure that rules are reasonable, agreed to, and accepted by all students. In this case, the core question would be if chewing gum is really a serious infraction worthy of a rule against it at all.

Talking above students' voices while giving directions or conducting instruction. A contemporary classroom manager wants to ensure that there is mutual respect among all class members. The teacher respects the students by listening to them when they speak; the students respect the teacher by listening when s/he speaks; the students respect each other by listening when they speak.

If there is not this cooperation, the teacher should determine why this is so. Are the students bored? Was their attention secured before the teacher or anyone else began to speak? Do the students understand the goals and objectives of instruction? Are there other underlying causes? The noise level in the classroom will intensify if you keep teaching or giving directions while the students are talking and not paying attention. But when students are actively engaged in productive group work, you can expect a reasonable noise level in the classroom.

Employing top-down communication in your classroom instead of facilitating the free and open interchange of ideas and suggestions. Authoritarian approaches to classroom management turn off students and have no place in the classroom of a contemporary manager. It was already indicated earlier in this chapter that an authoritative as opposed to an authoritarian style is much more effective in dealing with students.

An authoritarian teacher makes all the rules with no input from students. An authoritative teacher establishes rules through discussion with students. While infractions are met with consequences, they are not punishing in nature. The authoritative style is characterized by warmth, consistency, and mutually discussed and selected rules and is the recommended style according to the research (Marzano, 2003a).

Setting up an instructional system involving rote learning, drudgery, lack of student participation, and lack of variety. Be aware of instruction you provide that may involve these negative attributes. In addition to the fact that these negative approaches do not promote student achievement, students not engaged in meaningful activities will seek their own stimulation and find ways to become disruptive.

Ignoring students' strengths and emphasizing failures. Capitalizing on students' strengths leads to success. This success stimulates further motivation to achieve and reduces the desire for students to become disruptive.

Teachers should be aware of the fact that students' belief systems can affect success or failure. If students believe that failing means they are stupid, they are likely to adopt many self-protective, but also self-defeating, strategies. Just telling students to "try harder" is not particularly effective. Students need real evidence that effort will pay off, that setting a higher goal will not lead to failure, that they can improve, and that abilities can be changed. They need authentic mastery experiences. (Woolfolk, 2008, p. 431)

The above is a typical example of the strong connection between instruction and classroom management. The contemporary classroom manager helps students set instructional goals, demonstrates what goal mastery looks like, finds ways to demonstrate a student's progress, provides suggestions for improvement, emphasizes the link between past efforts and past accomplishments, and confronts directly self-defeating strategies (Woolfolk, 2008).

Requiring busy work. This type of assignment is unproductive and particularly irking to students, especially when the busy work, or any other assignment for that matter, is not returned. Teachers should constantly reflect on their assignments to make sure that they are meaningful.

Giving the same activities and assignments to all students instead of being selective according to need. Students who have instructional and procedural assignments that will tend to lead to success have fewer opportunities to become off-task and disruptive.

Inconsistency. Some teachers are inconsistent in implementing procedures. Sometimes teachers will allow calling out; other times they will insist that hands be raised. It becomes confusing to students when teachers do not enforce rules and procedures in the same way all the time.

Being consistent, insistent, and persistent makes students feel secure (Canter, 2006). They know what to expect when a question is asked, when they have to ask permission to perform a certain activity, and how to complete assignments.

Schools that experienced discipline problems did so when rules were unclear, perceived by students as unfair, not believed in by students, misconduct was ignored, teachers/administrators did not know or disagreed about the rules, and teachers' attitudes tended to be punitive (Washburn, Stowe, Cole, & Robinson, 2007).

It should be noted that consistency does *not* mean inflexibility. As stated earlier, there may be times when you need to reflect on procedures and change, with student input, those that may not be effective.

REACTIVE APPROACHES TO CLASSROOM MANAGEMENT

Even though you may have exhausted all the preventive measures just described, classroom misbehavior problems will still occur. How you handle misbehavior once it does occur is important in avoiding its recurrence. Remember that as a contemporary classroom manager, whenever possible, your reaction to behavior problems should be *educative* and should reinforce current recommended practices.

EDUCATIONAL INTERVENTION TECHNIQUES FOR HANDLING STUDENT MISBEHAVIOR

As stated previously, student ownership of all phases of managing the classroom offers the key to success. Effective practices in fostering this ownership consist of student input; shared responsibility; student autonomy, control, and involvement; self- regulation; and self-reflection. In addition, whenever misbehavior occurs, you should immediately analyze whether the students involved understand their role in a positive and supportive classroom environment and the goals/objectives of instruction and are engaged in meaningful activities.

When handling misbehavior problems:

Emphasize positive behavior. You may emphasize positive behavior in several ways.

Contrast the following two teacher statements addressed to Nicole and Martha regarding *Nicole's* misbehavior, who in this case is not paying attention.

> Statement 1: "Nicole, stop fiddling with your makeup case and pay attention."
> Statement 2: "Martha, I like the way you're paying attention and ready for the lesson."

In the first statement, the teacher tells Nicole how to behave. In the second statement, the teacher rewards (praises) Martha's positive behavior in the attempt to alert Nicole to the behavior she is supposed to be demonstrating. Even though Statement 2 is more effective than Statement 1, it is a traditional approach. Note that in addition to praise, the teacher is also using an "I" message in which s/he is exercising control.

There are some educators who believe that praise as used in the previous example is judgmental and can be problematic (Kohn, 1993, 2001; Tauber, 1999). They see praise as manipulative. It is something teachers do to students to get them to cooperate rather than engage them in a discussion of more important topics, such as what makes a good classroom work well or how what they do or neglect to do affects other class members.

Praise may increase students' dependence on the teacher, may cause students to lose interest, and as a result, reduce achievement. Using too much praise is ineffective in getting students to become self-managed because it informs the students that they should behave properly not for their own sake but to please you. However, you will recall from chapter 2 that Dreikurs (1998) promoted the practice of praising *effort* rather than performance because effort is within the student's control whereas physical dexterity and innate ability that could lead to higher performance levels are not.

A different way of emphasizing positive behavior is through *behavioral narration* in which you state the behavior of students who are complying with rules and/or procedures (Canter, 2006). Behavioral narration is *descriptive.* In Statement 2 p, you would use behavioral narration to describe what Martha is doing. "Martha is paying attention and ready for the lesson." Another example is, "Juanita has cleared her desk and her eyes are on me."

Yet another way to highlight the positive is by stating the behavior the misbehaving student *should* be demonstrating. It is more useful to make a positive statement such as, "Hank, your pad should be away," instead of making a negative statement such as, "Don't doodle during class."

A more contemporary approach to dealing with Hank's misbehavior is to ask him, "What are you doing to prevent our class from making progress?" He might answer, "I should put my pad away" or "I should stop doodling."

Whenever possible, your reaction should aim at *increasing student responsibility*. It is best to remind students of rules *they* have participated in constructing (assuming that you have done so at the beginning of the school year) and have them decide which rules are not being followed and then what to do about it.

Example:

> "Louis, look at the rule chart our class came up with and tell me which one you are now violating to hold up the class." Or you could simply have Louis just verbalize what he is doing to hold up the class. "I should clear my desk." You might also keep looking at Louis while pointing to the rule as you continue instruction without interruption.

State positive outcomes for correcting the misbehavior. When the student behaves appropriately, there will be a positive result.

Example:

"When you get back into your seat, Georgette, it will be your turn to guide our smartboard."

"When you get back into your seat, Georgette, our class will be able to continue to work on the projects they enjoy."

Request that a student state or put in writing what current misbehavior s/he is demonstrating. Some students are unaware that they are misbehaving (Glasser, 1975). Stating or writing the misbehavior brings it to a student's consciousness so that s/he can then correct the misbehavior.

Example:

"What are you doing, Jack?"

At first Jack might say, "Uh, nothing."

Then you would ask the question again. "What are you doing, Jack?"

"I am poking Juan."

"What should you be doing?"

"I should be paying attention."

Rearrange seating. If you find that some students have become overfriendly in class, break up the seating pattern. If the students have become overfriendly while working in groups, change the group structure. Twenty-first-century classroom managers know that noncompliance is a *symptom*. You will want to analyze why that symptom is occurring and what can be done to remedy the situation.

Remain calm. Quietly remind the class or a particular student that work is being held up. Avoid yelling (Tate, 2007). Yelling tells students that you are out of control, that you have "lost your cool." There are some students who enjoy getting the teacher to this state, and if you show you have reached it, they will repeat the same pattern that reinforces *your* behavior. The angrier a student becomes, the calmer you need to be. Your calmness serves as a stimulus that will help calm his/her anger (MacKenzie, 1996).

It is difficult but imperative to maintain emotional objectivity. To keep this objectivity at a high level, the teacher should avoid finger pointing, ridiculing, glaring at, or hovering over the offending student as well as raising the tone of voice with him/her. These behaviors should be replaced with keeping an appropriate distance from the student, speaking directly to him/her in a respectful way, looking directly without staring, and exhibiting a neutral or positive facial expression (Marzano, 2007).

Another related point is to avoid arguments with students. If you make the students the enemy, they will win (Rigsbee, 2008). When arguments occur, the class should first decide how to handle them. Assuming that their decision is reasonable, you should abide by it. Here again, you could ask the misbehaving student what s/he should be doing. You could also just stand firm and keep repeating *calmly* the behavior you want a student to demonstrate until s/he does so (Walker, Ramsey, & Gresham, 2004). "Carlos, sit down and open your book." "Carlos, sit down and open your book." "Carlos, sit down and open your book."

Keep the flow of the lesson while making minor corrections. You want to keep the momentum going by avoiding unnecessary interruptions, thus providing a cause for more disruptions. The more subtle your reaction, the better the chance that you will not have breaks in instruction.

Examples:

Call on a student who is not paying attention. You should do this in a nonthreatening way as a casual reminder that s/he is supposed to be paying attention.

Use the student's name in context during the lesson. Read the following approaches:

"Maureen, it's time for you to listen."

"When we analyzed this problem yesterday, Maureen, we came up with some criteria."

In the second approach, you reminded Maureen to pay attention without losing the momentum or content of the lesson.

Keep in physical contact with everyone in the class. Some teachers seem to be glued to the front of the room, especially during whole class instruction. They remain in the same position during the lesson, often standing at the board. Group focus, the suggestion of Kounin (1970) that you read earlier to prevent behavior problems, can also be used once they occur. Anticipate where trouble is brewing by moving to that section of the room. Conduct the class there for a while; then move to another area.

If a lot of board work is required during the lesson, train students to do some of the writing for you, leaving you free to move about, or prepare overheads or PowerPoint displays in advance and let the students operate the equipment at your direction as you circulate around the room.

If a student is playing with an object on the desk, move over to that student, *gently* remove the object from his/her hand, and put it where it belongs while keeping the discussion going. This technique is more successful than interrupting the lesson to say, "Doreen, put that eraser away."

If a Student or Students Begin Speaking While You Are Speaking, Interrupt Your Sentence during a Word at the End of a Syl . . . Did that just get your attention?

Silence is likely to follow stopping your sentence in the middle of a word (at the end of a syllable). Silence is a powerful attention-getter, and once you have that silence, you can continue speaking. This approach is more subtle and effective than stopping the lesson and saying, "Will everyone stop talking and pay attention?" or "I want everyone to stop talking and pay attention."

Another approach is to keep talking and gradually lower your voice.

As a shared leader in a learning community, you can express YOUR feeling about a misbehavior. A specific type of "I" message introduced by Gordon (1974) is still being used today to communicate effectively your feelings to misbehaving students. This specific "I" message is different from the one previously introduced in this chapter. Gordon's message has three parts. It states what the misbehavior is, the tangible effect that misbehavior has on you, and how it makes you feel.

Examples: "When you call out answers (misbehavior), it makes it difficult for me to keep everyone in the class involved (effect on you), and I feel disappointed that I'm not doing my job properly (how you feel)."

"When you keep taking pencils from my desk (misbehavior), I can't keep track of how many I have for the other students (effect on you), and I feel frustrated (how you feel)."

A modification of the above "I" message was offered by Canter and Canter (1992). They suggested that the "I" message be reversed. The Canters' version begins with the teacher's feeling, then the misbehavior, and finally what behavior the teacher wants instead.

Example: "I feel I'm not doing my job properly (teacher's feeling) when you call out answers (misbehavior), and I want you to raise your hand if you want to participate in the discussion (behavior the teacher wants)."

This "I" message can be more in keeping with contemporary approaches by saying, "I feel I'm not doing my job properly (teacher's feeling) when you call out answers (misbehavior), and as the class decided, you should raise your hand if you want to participate in the discussion (behavior agreed to by both class and teacher)."

Remember that when using "You" messages (referred to in table 4.1), the student's behavior is being reinforced. When using "I" messages, you are correcting misbehavior by expressing your feelings.

Use nonverbal communication to keep students' attention. Direct eye contact with a student will redirect his/her attention. While conducting the lesson, you could also keep looking (not staring) at a student who is not looking at you or not behaving appropriately. The other students are likely to signal him/her that you are looking, which in turn should alert him/her to refocus attention on work.

You could turn off or flicker the lights, or ring a bell to regain attention. Raising your hand or your brow, nodding or shaking your head, or placing your finger over your lips may also help. With younger children you can use the game, Statue, and say, "Freeze." Students at early grade levels respond well to this command.

You could also begin clapping in a different rhythm each time you want attention. Advise, teach, and practice with the students in advance so that whenever you do this, they should stop whatever they are doing, listen to the rhythm, and clap in the same rhythm. However, whichever stimulus you choose should be *varied*, for if you repeat the same stimulus constantly, the students will become conditioned to it and eventually ignore it.

At this juncture, it would be suitable to reinforce the fact that only about 7 percent of communication comes through the spoken word. Body gestures, voice tone, facial expressions, and general posture communicate the rest. These nonverbal messages mean different things to students from different cultures, especially when there is a nonmatch between the spoken word and the body language. Since eye contact, gestures, physical proximity, as well as physical contact are interpreted differently, you must learn as much as you can about the various cultures represented in your class and act accordingly (McGee, 2008).

Have individual conferences with students who are constantly behaving improperly. If you make a case of students' misbehavior in front of the class, you may reinforce the misbehavior. Class members behave very differently individually from the way they do in groups. Students, adolescents in particular, try to maintain a high social status with their peers, making them defensive and creating difficulty for you to discover what the problem actually is.

Plan your conference by carefully structuring the questions you want to ask. Some examples are as follows: "Is there anything I am doing that causes you to react the way you do in class?" "Is there a way I could improve the class to make it more interesting for you?" "Are you having a problem I could help you with?"

Sometimes, asking that student to state if *you* are doing something to cause the misbehavior can be revealing. The student could be surprised that you asked the question and may realize for the first time that his/her behavior is affecting you. The student may actually tell you if you are doing something that bothers him/her and may suggest other topics of interest and/or other ways of learning or being evaluated.

Also, just as people who work in industry recognize that sharing ideas over a business lunch improves communication with customers and increases sales, sharing a one-to-one meal with a chronically misbehaving student can promote a more positive relationship with that student and foster improved cooperation on his/her part.

Apply logical consequences. In keeping with making the students responsible for their own behavior, it is an effective procedure to apply logical consequences for misbehavior (Glasser, 1975). Logical consequences are educative. They are not the same as punishment because they are directly connected to the misbehavior and hold the student accountable while maintaining his/her dignity (Gootman, 1997).

Logical consequences should not be packaged as logical consequences but should be *really* logical (Kohn, 1996). They should have some conceptual connection to the student's behavior.

Examples: A student who punches another student (misbehavior) must make a list of alternative ways to settle disputes (logical consequence).

A student who draws graffiti on a wall (misbehavior) must clean it (logical consequence).

Use peers to correct misbehavior. Try to keep the level of engagement and motivation so high in your classroom that the other students themselves will tend to correct the disrupters. This approach will be more successful if students have been empowered to share responsibility with you for instruction and for classroom management. Whenever possible, have the students decide what to do about a person who is (constantly) disrupting the class.

A useful variation of using peers is using *reverse modeling*. Have a student who is misbehaving model the *correct* behavior for the other students.

Example:

"Harry (the student who is fooling around instead of getting ready to leave), show the class what to do to get ready for dismissal." See Table 4.3 for best practices criteria for classroom management.

More Challenging Cases

There will always be some behavioral situations that will be more challenging.

Some situations may not be conducive to handling them by yourself; you might have to seek the help of a specialist. Keep in mind that misbehavior was symptomatic and that the *only* exception where a student could not control behavior involved organic disorders (Canter, 2006).

Now that you have reviewed some of the ways to deal with misbehavior problems, consider how a caring classroom atmosphere in which students interact with each other and with other students positively might have prevented aggressive behaviors from reaching that stage.

The National Education Association (NEA) reports other demanding situations on their website (http://www.nea.org). These include dealing with the class clown, recalcitrant students, and fighting students. Remember that these disruptive behaviors will have much less of an opportunity to flourish if you have built a sense of community in your class. As you read through the following section, *think of how the following occurrences (symptoms) could be avoided or at least mitigated if students in your class support and feet responsible for each other.*

The class clown. This student uses joking as an attention-seeking device. In many cases, s/he is successful and this success serves as a stimulant for further clowning. As a twenty-first-century classroom manager, first ask yourself why this behavior is occurring. How involved is this student? How successful is s/he? What can be done to improve his/her achievement?

Then ask the class for their input by saying, "We have decided to achieve these goals together. How is _____ interfering with our success?" "How is _____'s behavior interfering with his/her success?" Then, "What is the best way to deal with this situation?" If the class cannot handle this behavior, the NEA suggests that without direct eye contact you could approach the student who is clowning and warn him/her about possible isolation. If the warning does not stop the misbehavior, move the student to a different part of the classroom for a brief time.

Recalcitrant students. If a student is noncompliant, the teacher should analyze why the student is refusing to do the assigned work. If the class cannot help solve the situation, try doing some of the work with the student. While working together, the NEA recommends that you discuss the assignment to see if the student understands it and can find some motivation in it. Remind the student of similar (or any) assignments in which s/he experienced success. If necessary, have the student select a different task with a similar goal or objective before returning to the original assignment.

At any sign of beginning the assignment, offer the student encouragement. Communicate high expectations for effort by saying something similar to, "Rule #1 is that everyone must participate. That means 100 percent. The

Table 4.3. Best Practices for Effective Classroom Management (T)

Proactive Phase: Effective Classroom Management Practices to Prevent Problems	
Criteria (Descriptors)	*Performance Indicators (Examples)*
The teacher implemented an engaging instructional system with a variety of approaches and assessments	
conveyed and implemented expectation that all would support each other to succeed	
established with input from students (when age appropriate) no more than eight brief clear rules stated in positive terms	
secured student input regarding rewards for following rules and consequences for not following rules	
shared with students the responsibility for implementing and enforcing rules	
established with input from students (when age appropriate) procedures to make the class run smoothly	
practiced rules/procedures with class	
implemented rules/procedures consistently	
called each student by name	
evidenced awareness of what each student was doing all the time	
managed transitions from one activity to another smoothly	
demonstrated respect for each student	
worked unpopular students into groups and lessons	
interacted with students in a friendly but businesslike manner	
used "You" messages to reinforce positive work and behavior	
reflected to identify any teacher-caused student misbehavior problems	
established with class input *improved* procedures/ routines/classroom setup, and so on as a result of analyzing less efficient past practices	
Reactive Phase: Effective Classroom Management Practices to Handle Problems Once they have Occurred	
Criteria (Descriptors)	*Performance Indicators (Examples)*
The teacher remained calm waited for attention	

Reactive Phase: Effective Classroom Management Practices to Handle Problems Once they have Occurred	
Criteria (Descriptors)	*Performance Indicators (Examples)*
involved the class first in solving the problem, when appropriate	
used nonverbal signals	
moved immediately to area of disruption	
used any misbehaving student's name *in context*	
used behavioral narration	
removed any interfering physical object(s) casually without breaking the flow of instruction	
reassigned seating to misbehaving student(s)	
recognized behavior opposite the misbehavior	
used "I" messages	
applied naturally occurring (logical) consequences	
addressed misbehaving student(s) personally and privately	
requested that a misbehaving student state or write the misbehavior	

Ineffective Classroom Management Practices (Those to be Eliminated)	
Criteria (Descriptors)	*Performance Indicators (Examples)*
The teacher used authoritarian methods to control the class	
spoke over students' voices	
exhibited favoritism	
demonstrated resentment toward student(s)	
made a sarcastic or other inappropriate remark(s) or gestures	
assigned busy work	
implemented rules and routines inconsistently	
discussed with colleagues if any changes (modifications, additions, deletions) were needed in the above effective or ineffective criteria as a result of new research	

reason our class set up this rule is that the more we participate, the more we achieve. We don't use words as can't or won't. At least try, and if you need help, you'll get it" (National Education Association, 2009).

Students get involved in fights. Sometimes students have arguments, which can accelerate into fights. Some basic techniques for breaking up fights and dealing with physically aggressive students are offered by Johns and Carr

(1995). They suggest that small acts of aggression can escalate into more violent acts. Therefore, do not ignore aggression.

Since frequently the mere presence of an adult will stop a potentially violent act, move toward the violent scene. Review the situation quickly to determine who is involved and what may likely happen.

If gangs are involved, send a nonparticipant for more adults. Check for weapons. Because students sometimes hope that an adult will tell them to stop fighting to give them a "graceful" way to bow out, tell students in a strong voice to stop. Tell onlookers to leave. Make a mental note of the onlookers. If you know any of these observers by name, address them *by name* and tell them where to go.

Inform observers and those involved in the fighting the consequences of not following your directions. NEVER get in between fighting students. Tell the students to stop in a loud, demanding voice, remembering that many times students will welcome an excuse to quit. When the incident is over, document what happened and share this information with others, as required. Most important, as soon as possible after the incident is over, get professional help for both victims and aggressors.

If all of the proactive and reactive suggestions you have read seem overwhelming, be confident in the fact that implementing successful classroom management is an art, which incorporates many different strategies and, as with all other skills, takes *time* to master. The more you practice these strategies in your classroom, the more adept you will be at recognizing when they will be effective and how to apply them.

References

Albergaria-Almeida, P. (2010). Classroom questioning: Teachers' perceptions and practices. *Procedia-Social and Behavioral Sciences, 2*(2), 305–09.

American Association of University Women. (1992). *How schools short-change girls: The AAUW report*. Washington, DC: AAUW Educational Foundation.

Ausubel, D. (1963). *The psychology of meaningful verbal learning*. New York: Grune & Stratton.

Ausubel, D. (1977). The facilitation of meaningful verbal learning in the classroom. *Educational Psychologist, 12*(2), 162–178.

Ausubel, D., Novak, J., & Hanesian, H. (1978). *Educational psychology: A cognitive view*. New York: Holt, Rinehart, & Winston.

Bandura, A. (1969). *Principles of behavior modification*. New York: Holt, Rinehart, & Winston.

Bandura, A. (Ed.). (1974). *Psychological modeling: Conflicting theories*. New York: Lieber-Atherton.

Bandura, A. (1986). *Social foundations of thought and action*. Englewood Cliffs, NJ: Prentice-Hall.

Bandura, A., & Walters, R. (1963). *Social learning and personality development*. New York: Holt, Rinehart, & Winston.

Beane, A. (1999). *The bully free classroom: Over 100 tips and strategies for teachers K-8*. Minneapolis, MN: Free Spirit Publishing.

Benjafield, J. (1992). *Cognition*. Englewood Cliffs, NJ: Prentice Hall.

Black, S. (2001). Ask me a question: How teachers use inquiry in the classroom. *American School Board Journal, 188*(5), 43–45.

Bloom, B. (1968). Learning for mastery. *Evaluation Comment, 1*(2). Los Angeles, CA: University of California, Center for the Study of Evaluation of Instructional Programs.

Bloom, B. (1976). *Human characteristics and school learning*. New York: McGraw-Hill.

Borich, G. (2007). *Effective teaching methods: Research-based practice* (6th ed.). Upper Saddle River, NJ: Pearson/Merrill Prentice Hall.

Bowers, C., & Flinders, D. (1991). *Culturally responsive teaching and supervision: A handbook for staff development*. New York: Teachers College Press.

Boynton, M., & Boynton, C. (2005). *The educator's guide to preventing and solving discipline problems*. Alexandria, VA: Association for Supervision and Curriculum Development.

Brookhart, S. (2004). *Grading*. Upper Saddle River, NJ: Pearson Education.

Brooks, D. (2011). *The social animal: The hidden sources of love, character, and achievement*. New York: Random House.

Brophy, J. (1979). *Teacher praise: A functional analysis*. Occasional paper No. 2. East Lansing, MI: Michigan State University, Institute for Research on Teaching.

Brophy, J., & Evertson, C. (1976). *Learning from teaching: A developmental perspective*. Boston, MA: Allyn & Bacon.

Bruner, J. (1961). *The process of education*. Cambridge, MA: Harvard University Press.

Cangelosi, J. (2008). *Classroom management strategies: Gaining and maintaining students' cooperation* (6th ed.). Hoboken, NJ: John Wiley & Sons.

Canter, L. (2006). *Classroom management for academic success*. Bloomington, IN: Solution Tree.

Canter, L., & Canter, M. (1992). *Assertive discipline*. Santa Monica, CA: Canter & Associates.

Canter, L., & Canter, M. (2001). *Assertive discipline: Positive behavior management for today's classrooms* (3rd ed.). Santa Monica, CA: Canter & Associates.

Carroll, J. (1963). A model of school learning. *Teachers College Record, 64*, 722–33.

Chetty, R., Friedman, J., & Rockoff, J. (2012, January). *The long-term impacts of teachers: Teacher value-added and student outcomes in adulthood* (NBER Working Paper No. 17699, JEL No. I2, J24).

Chuska, K. R. (1995). *Improving classroom questions*. Bloomington, IN: Phi Delta Kappa.

Cotton, K. (2000). *The schooling practices that matter most*. Alexandria, VA: Association for Supervision and Curriculum Development.

Cruickshank, D., Bainer Jenkins, D, & Metcalf, K. (2003). *The act of teaching* (3rd ed.). Boston, MA: McGraw-Hill.

Cummings, C. (2000). *Winning strategies for classroom management*. Alexandria, VA: Association for Supervision and Curriculum Development.

Curwin, R., & Mendler, A. (1999). *Discipline with dignity* (2nd ed.). Alexandria, VA: Association for Supervision and Curriculum Development.

Danielson, C. (1996). *Enhancing professional practice: A framework for teaching*. Alexandria, VA: Association for Supervision and Curriculum Development.

Danielson, C. (2007). *Enhancing professional practice: A framework for teaching* (2nd ed.). Alexandria, VA: Association for Supervision and Curriculum Development.

Danielson, C. (2008). *Handbook for enhancing professional practice: Using the framework for teaching in your school*. Alexandria, VA: Association for Supervision and Curriculum Development.

Danielson, C. (2016, April 20). Rethinking teacher evaluation. *Education Week*, *35*(28), 20, 24.

Danielson, C., & McGreal, T. (2000). *Teacher evaluation to enhance professional practice*. Alexandria, VA: Association for Supervision and Curriculum Development.

Davis, G. (1983). *Educational psychology: Theory and practice*. Reading, MA: Addison-Wesley.

Delpit, L. (1995). *Other people's children: Cultural conflict in the classroom*. New York: The New Press.

Dewey, J. (1916). *Democracy and education*. New York: Macmillan.

Dewey, J. (1938). *Experience and education*. New York: Collier.

Dillon, J. (1988). *Questioning and teaching*. New York: Teachers College Press.

Dreikurs, R. (1998). *Maintaining sanity in the classroom: Classroom management techniques* (2nd ed.). Washington, DC: Accelerated Development.

Drozynski, D., Furman, T., Ellis, J., Guertin, L. (2010, March). Using student questions to guide earth science inquiry in middle school. *The Geological Society of America*, Paper No. 49–2.

Dweck, C. (2008, Summer). The perils and promises of praise. *Educational Leadership*, *65*, 30–39.

Emmer, E., Evertson, C., & Worsham, M. (2003a). *Classroom management for elementary teachers* (6th ed.). Boston, MA: Allyn & Bacon.

Emmer, E., Evertson, C., & Worsham, M. (2003b). *Classroom management for secondary teachers* (6th ed.). Boston, MA: Allyn & Bacon.

Engel, S., & Sandstrom, M. (2010, July 22). There's only one way to stop a bully. *The New York Times*, A23.

Ericksen, S. (1978). *The lecture: Memo to the faculty*, no. 60. Ann Arbor, MI: Center for Research on Teaching and Learning, University of Michigan.

Evertson, C., & Weinstein, C. (Eds.). (2006). *Handbook of classroom management: Research, practice, and contemporary issues*. Mahwah, NJ: Erlbaum.

Fay, J., & Funk, D. (1995). *Teaching with love and logic*. Golden, CO: Love & Logic Press.

Felch, J., Song, J., & Poindexter, S. (2010, December 22). In reforming schools, quality of teaching often overlooked. *Los Angeles Times*, p. 4.

Franklin, J. (2006, March). The essential ounce of prevention: Effective classroom management means more than intervention. *Education Update*, *48*(3), 3–8. Association for Supervision and Curriculum Development.

Frisby, B., & Martin, M. (2010, April). Instructor-student and student-student rapport in the classroom. *Communication Education*, *59*(2), 146–64.

Fryshman, B. (2014, August 11). Let's be honest: We don't know how to make great teachers. *Education Week* Online. http://www.edweek.org/tm/articles/2014/08/11/fp_fryshman_teacher_quality.html

Gagne, E., Yekovick, C., & Yekovick, F. (1993). *The cognitive psychology of school learning* (2nd ed.). New York: HarperCollins.

Gall, M., Gall, J., & Borg, W. (2003). *Educational research: An introduction* (7th ed.). Boston, MA: Allyn & Bacon.

Gammill, A. (2010, May 21). IPS teacher goes from mutiny to best in class. Indystar.com.

98 *References*

Glasser, W. (1975). *Reality therapy: A new approach to psychiatry*. New York: Harper & Row.

Good, T. (1996). Teacher effects and teacher evaluation. In J. Sikula (Ed.), *Handbook of research on teacher education* (pp. 617–65). New York: Macmillan.

Good, T., & Brophy, J. (1974). Changing teacher and student behavior: An empirical investigation. *Journal of Educational Psychology, 66,* 390–405.

Good, T., & Brophy, J. (1997). *Looking in classrooms* (7th ed.). New York: Longman.

Good, T., & Brophy, J. (2003). *Looking in classrooms,* 9th ed. Boston: Allyn & Bacon.

Gootman, M. (1997). *The caring teacher's guide to discipline*. Thousand Oaks, CA: Corwin Press.

Gordon, T. (1974). *Teacher effectiveness training*. New York: Peter H. Weyden.

Haber, J. (2007). *Bullyproof your child for life: Protect your child from teasing, taunting, and bullying for good*. New York: Penguin/Perigee.

Hall, E. (1977). *Beyond culture*. Garden City, NY: Anchor.

Hanson, J. (1998). *Classroom management: An ASCD professional inquiry kit*. Alexandria, VA: Association for Supervision and Curriculum Development.

Hanushek, E. (2011, April 6). Recognizing the value of good teachers. *Education Week, 30*(27), 34–35.

Haycock, K. (1998). Good teaching matters . . . a lot. *Thinking K-16, 3*(2), 1–14.

Hook, C., & Rosenshine, B. (1979). Accuracy of teacher reports of their classroom behavior. *Review of Educational Research, 49,* 1–12.

Hoover, J., & Oliver, R. (1996). *The bullying prevention handbook: A guide for principals, teachers, and counselors*. Bloomington, IN: National Educational Service.

Hunter, R. (2004). *Madeline Hunter's mastery teaching: Increasing instructional effectiveness in elementary and secondary schools* (Updated ed.). Thousand Oaks, CA: Corwin Press.

Hutchings, P., & Wurtzdorff, A. (1988). Experiential learning across the curriculum: Assumptions and principles. In P. Hutchings & A. Wurtzdorff (eds.), *New Directions for Teaching and Learning,* no. 35, pp 198–227. San Francisco: Jossey-Bass.

Interstate New Teacher Assessment and Support Consortium (INTASC). (1995). *Next steps: Moving toward performance-based licensing in teaching*. Washington, DC: Author.

Jensen, E. (1998). *Teaching with the brain in mind*. Alexandria, VA: Association for Supervision and Curriculum Development.

Jensen, E. (2005). *Teaching with the brain in mind* (2nd ed.). Alexandria, VA: Association for Supervision and Curriculum Development.

Johns, B., & Carr, V. (1995). *Techniques for managing verbally and physically aggressive students*. Columbia, MO: Hawthorne Educational Services.

Jones, V., & Jones, L. (2003). *Comprehensive classroom management: Creating communities of support and solving problems* (7th ed.). Boston, MA: Allyn & Bacon.

Joyce, B., & Showers, B. (1995). *Student achievement through staff development* (2nd ed.). New York: Longman.

Joyce, B, & Showers, B. (2002). *Student achievement through staff development* (3rd ed.). Alexandria, VA: Association for Supervision and Curriculum Development.

Joyce B., & Weil, M. (2000). *Models of teaching* (6th ed.). Needham Heights, MA: Allyn & Bacon.

Joyce, B., Weil, M., with Calhoun, E. (2004). *Models of teaching* (7th ed.). Boston, MA: Pearson.

Juvonen, J., Graham, S., & Schuster, M. (2003). Bullying among young adolescents: The strong, the weak, and the troubled. *Pediatrics, 112*, 1231–37.

King, A., & Rosenshine, B. (1993). Effects of guided cooperating questions on children's knowledge constructed. *Journal of Experimental Education, 61*(2), 27–148.

Kohn, A. (1993). *Punished by rewards.* Boston, MA: Houghton Mifflin.

Kohn, A. (1996). *Beyond discipline: From compliance to community.* Alexandria, VA: Association for Supervision and Curriculum Development.

Kohn, A. (2001, September). Five reasons to stop saying "good job." *Young Children.* http://www.alfiekohn.org

Kohn, A. (2003, March). Almost there, but not quite. *Educational Leadership, 58*(3), 20–24.

Kohn, A. (2008). Why self-discipline is overrated: The (troubling) theory and practice of control from within. *Phi Delta Kappan, 90*(3), 168–76.

Kottler, J., Zehm, S., & Kottler, E. (2005). *On becoming a teacher: The human dimension* (3rd ed.). Thousand Oaks, CA: Corwin Press.

Kounin, J. (1970). *Discipline and group management in classrooms.* New York: Holt, Rinehart, & Winston.

Labaree, D. (2008). An easy relationship: A history of teacher education in the university. In Cochran-Smith, M., Feiman-Nemser, S., & McIntyre, J. (Eds.). *Handbook of Research on Teacher Education: Enduring Questions in Changing Contexts* (3rd ed.). (pp. 290–306). New York: Routledge.

Lee, V., Chen, X., & Smerdon, B. (1996). *The influence of school climate on gender differences in the achievement and engagement of young adolescents.* Washington, DC: American Association of University Women.

Long, J., & Frye, V. (1985). *Making it till Friday: A guide to successful classroom management* (3rd ed.). Princeton, NJ: Princeton Book Company.

MacKenzie, R. (1996). *Setting limits in the classroom: How to move beyond the classroom dance of discipline.* Roseville, CA: Prima.

Marks, M. (2000, January 9). Education Life. *The New York Times*, pp. 16–17.

Marzano, R. (2003a). *What works in schools?* Alexandria, VA: Association for Supervision and Curriculum Development.

Marzano, R. (2003b). *Classroom management that works.* Alexandria, VA: Association for Supervision and Curriculum Development.

Marzano, R. (2007). *The art and science of teaching: A comprehensive framework for effective instruction.* Alexandria, VA: Association for Supervision and Curriculum Development.

Marzano, R. (2017). *The new art and science of teaching.* Bloomington, IN: Solution Tree Press.

Marzano, R., Pickering, D., & Pollock, J. (2001). *Classroom instruction that works: Research-based strategies for increasing student achievement.* Alexandria, VA: Association for Supervision and Curriculum Development.

McGee, K. (2008). How cultural differences may affect student performance. *Great Schools.* http://www.greatschools.net

McLeod, J., Fisher, J., & Hoover, G. (2003). *The key elements of classroom management: Managing time and space, student behavior, and instructional strategies.* Alexandria, VA: Association for Supervision and Curriculum Development.

McLeskey, J., & Waldron, N. (2004). Three conceptions of teacher learning: Exploring the relationship between knowledge and the practice of teaching. *Teacher Education and Special Education, 27*(1), 3–14.

Michaelis, J. (1963). *Social studies for children in a democracy.* Englewood Cliffs, NJ: Prentice-Hall.

Miller, N., & Dollard, J. (1941). *Social learning and imitation.* New Haven, CT: Yale University Press.

National Commission on Teaching and America's Future. (1996). *What matters most: Teaching for America's future.* New York: Carnegie Foundation, Author.

National Education Association (2009). http://www.nea.org/home/ToolsAndIdeas.html

Newman, R., & Schwager, M. (1993). Students' perception of the teacher and classmates in relation to reported help seeking in math class. *The Elementary School Journal, 94*(1), 3–17.

Nye, B., Konstantopoulos, S., & Hedges, L. (2004, Fall). How large are teacher effects? *Educational Evaluation and Policy Analysis, 26*(3), 237–57.

Oakes, J., & Lipton, M. (2003). *Teaching to change the world* (2nd ed.). New York: McGraw-Hill.

Oliveira, A. (2010, April). Improving teacher questioning in science inquiry discussions through professional development. *Journal of Research in Science Teaching, 47*(4), 422–53.

Orloff, S. (2008). The whole child. *Exceptional Parent, 38*(5), 48–49.

Pagliaro, M. (2011). *Differentiating instruction: Matching strategies with objectives.* Lanham, MD: Rowman & Littlefield.

Pagliaro, M. (2012). *Research-based unit and lesson planning: Maximizing student achievement.* Lanham, MD: Rowman & Littlefield.

Penner, J. (1984). *Why many college teachers cannot lecture.* Springfield, IL: Thomas.

Piaget, J. (1952). *The origins of intelligence in children.* New York: Basic Books

Piaget, J. (1954). *The construction of reality in the child* (M. Cook, Trans.). New York: Basic Books.

Pianta, R. (2007, November 6). Measure actual classroom teaching. *Education Week.* http://www.edweek.org/ew/articles/2007/11/07/11pianta.h27.html

Pipho, C. (1998, January). The value-added side of standards. *Phi Delta Kappan,* 341–42.

Ravitch, D. (2003, August 23). A brief history of teacher professionalism. White House Conference on Preparing Tomorrow's Teachers.

Resnick, L. (1987). *Education and learning to think.* Washington, DC: Academic Press.

Rieman, A., & Thies-Sprinthall, L. (1998). *Mentoring and supervision for teacher development.* New York: Longman.

Rigsbee, C. (2008, January). Positively teaching. *Teacher Magazine*. http://www. teachermagazine.org/tm/articles/2008/01/30/20tln_rigsbee_web.h19.html

Rodkin, P., Farmer, T., Pearl, R, & VanAcker, R. (2000). Heterogeneity of popular boys: Antisocial and prosocial configurations. *Developmental Psychology, 36*, 14–24.

Rosch, E. (1973). On the internal structure of perceptual and semantic categories. In T. Moore (Ed.), *Cognitive development and the acquisition of language* (pp. 111–44). New York: Academic Press.

Rowe, M. (1974). Wait-time and rewards as instructional variables, their influence on language, logic and fate control: Part one: Wait-Time. *Journal of Research in Science Teaching, 11*, 81–84.

Rowe, M. (1986, January/February). Wait time: Slowing down may be a way of speeding up! *Journal of Teacher Education, 37*(1), 43–50.

Ryan, K., Cooper, J., & Tauer, S. (2008). *Teaching for student learning: Becoming a master teacher*. Boston, MA: Houghton Mifflin.

Sackstein, S. (2016). Teachers vs Educators: Which Are You?—Work in Progress. http://blogs.edweek.org/teachers/work_in_progress/2016/05/teachers_vs_ educators_which_ar.html

Sadker, M., & Sadker, D. (1994). *Failing at fairness: How America's schools cheat girls*. New York: Scribner.

Sadker, M., & Sadker, D. (1997). *Teachers, schools, and society*. New York: McGraw-Hill.

Sanders, W., & Rivers, J. (1996). *Cumulative and residual effects of teachers on future student academic achievement*. Research progress report. Knoxville, TN: University of Tennessee Value-Added Research and Assessment Center.

Schneider, J. (2015, April 15). A national strategy to improve the teaching profession. *Education Week, 34*(27), 20–21.

Schwartz, B., & Reisberg, D. (1991). *Learning and memory*. New York: Norton.

Schunk, D. (1987). Peer models and children's behavioral change. *Review of Educational Research, 57*, 149–74.

Schunk, D. (2000). *Learning theories: An educational perspective* (3rd ed.). Columbus, OH: Merrill/Prentice Hall.

Schunk, D., & Hanson, A. (1985). Peer models: Influences on children's self-efficiency and achievement. *Journal of Educational Psychology, 77*, 313–22.

Scollon, R. (1985). The machine stops: Silence in the metaphor of malfunction. In D. Tannen & M. Saville-Troike (Eds.), *Perspectives on silence*. Norwood, NJ: Ablex.

Shah, N. (2011, February 8). Study disputes myth of school bullies' social status. *Education Week, 30*(21), 1, 12.

Siegman, A., & Feldstein, S. (Eds.). (1987). *Nonverbal behavior and communication*. Hillsdale, NJ: Erlbaum.

Sommers, C. (1996, June 12). Where the boys are. *Education Week*. http://educationweek.org

Starr, L. (2003). Are you a bully? EducationWorld.com.

Steinberg, L. (1996). *Beyond the classroom: Why school reform has failed and what parents need to do*. New York: Simon & Schuster.

Stepien, W., Johnson, T., & Checkley, K. (1997). *Problem-based learning, Facilitator's guide*. Alexandria, VA: Association for Supervision and Curriculum Development.

Stevens, R. (1912). The question as a measure of efficiency in instruction: A critical study of classroom practice. *Teachers College Contributions to Education, 48.* New York: Teachers College.

Taba, H. (1967). *Teacher's handbook for elementary school social studies.* Reading, MA: Addison Wesley.

Tate, M. (2007). *Shouting won't grow dendrites: 20 techniques for managing a brain-compatible classroom.* Thousand Oaks, CA: Corwin Press.

Tauber, R. (1999). *Classroom management: Sound theory and effective practice* (3rd ed.). Westport, CT: Bergin & Garvey.

Tauber, R. (2007). *Classroom management: Sound theory and effective practice* (4th ed.). Portsmouth, NH: Praeger.

Tedrow, M. (2008, May 28). Best practices: The miracle of choices. *Teacher Magazine.* http://www.teachermagazine.org

Thelen, H. (1960). *Education and the human quest.* New York: Harper and Row.

Tobias, S. (2008, August 22). Slowing speech eases a child's ability to listen. *The Wichita Eagle,* Examiner.com/National.

Tomlinson, C. (2001). *How to differentiate instruction in mixed-ability classrooms* (2nd ed.). Alexandria, VA: Association for Supervision and Curriculum Development.

Treffinger, D. (2008, Summer). Preparing creative and critical thinkers. *Educational Leadership 65.* Thinking skills NOW, Association for Supervision and Curriculum Development (online only).

Tucker, M. (2016, April 14). How to get a first-rate teacher in front of every student—Top performers. http://blogs.edweek.org/edweek/top_performers/2016/04.html

University of Florida. (2008, April 23). Social form of bullying linked to depression, anxiety in adults. *Science Daily.* Retrieved April 25, 2008 from http://www.sciencedaily.com/releases/2008/04/080422143529.htm

Viadero, D. (2010, May 19). Study sees broad view of bullying culture. *Education Week, 29*(32), 1, 18–29.

Vogler, K. (2008, Summer). Asking good questions. *Educational Leadership Online.*

Vygotsky, L. (1978). *Mind in society: The development of higher mental process.* Cambridge, MA: Harvard University Press.

Walker, H., Ramsey, E., & Gresham, F. (2004). *Antisocial behavior in school: Evidence-based practices* (2nd ed.). Belmont, CA: Wadsworth/Thomson.

Walsh, J., & Sattes, B. (2005). *Quality questioning: Research-based practice to engage every learner.* Thousand Oaks, CA: Corwin Press.

Wang, M., Haertel, G., & Walberg, H. (1993). Toward a knowledge base for school learning. *Review of Educational Research, 63*(3), 249–94.

Washburn, S., Stowe, K., Cole, C, & Robinson, J. (2007, Fall). Improving school climate and student behavior: A new paradigm for Indiana schools. Educational Policy Brief, *Center for Evaluation and Educational Policy, 5*(9).

Weiss, I., & Pasley, J. (2004). What is high-quality instruction? *Educational Leadership, 61*(5), 24–28.

West, P. (2009, June 29). Cyber bullying affects one in 10 students. *HealthDay Reporter.* http://abcnews.go.com/Health/Healthday/story?id=7960972.

White, R., & Tisher, R. (1986). Research on natural sciences. In M. C. Wittrock (Ed.), *Handbook of research on teaching* (3rd ed.), pp. 874–905. New York: Macmillan.

Wiener, R. (2016, April 26). Three strategies to improve teacher evaluation. *Education Week, 25*(29), 25, 28.

Wiggins, G. (1998). *Educative assessment: Designing assessments to inform and improve student performance*. San Francisco, CA: Jossey-Bass.

Wiggins, G. (2005). *Educative assessment* (2nd ed.). Alexandria, VA: Association for Supervision and Curriculum Development.

Wilen, W. (2001). Exploring myths about teacher questioning in the social studies classroom. *Social Studies, 92*(1), 26–32.

Wolfe, P. (2001). Brain research: Fad or foundation? Audiotape #201099. Alexandria, VA: Association for Supervision and Curriculum Development.

Wolvin, A. (1983). Improving listening skills. In R. B. Rubin (Ed.), *Improving speaking and listening skills: New directions for college learning assistance*, no. 12, pp. 78–93. San Francisco: Jossey-Bass.

Wong, H. (1989). *How you can be a successful teacher*. Sunnyvale, CA: Harry Wong Tapes.

Wong, H., & Wong, R. (1998). *The first days of school*. Mountain View, CA: Harry K. Wong Publications.

Wong, H., & Wong, R. (2005). The first days of school: How to be an effective teacher (3rd ed.). Mountain View, CA: Harry K. Wong Publications.

Woolfolk, A. (2008). *Educational psychology* (10th ed.). Boston, MA: Pearson.

Wragg, E. (1993). *Primary teaching skills*. London: Routledge.

Wragg, E., & Brown, G. (2001). *Questioning in the primary schools*. London: Routledge.

Wright, S., Horn, S., & Sanders, W. (1997). Teacher and classroom context effects on student achievement: Implications for teacher evaluation. *Journal of Personnel Evaluation in Education, 11*, 57–67.

Zhang, M., Lundeberg, M., McConnell, T., Koehler, M., & Eberhardt, J. (2010, January). Using questioning to facilitate discussion of science teaching problems in teacher professional development. *Interdisciplinary Journal of Problem-based Learning, 4*(1), 57–82.

About the Author

Marie Menna Pagliaro is currently a professional development consultant. She was a full professor and director of the Teacher Education Division at Dominican College, chair of the Education Department at Marymount College, a supervisor of student teachers at Lehman College of the City University of New York, and chair of the Science Department and teacher of chemistry, general science, and mathematics in the Yonkers Public Schools. She received her PhD in curriculum and teaching from Fordham University.